# PRESS BOX

# PRESS BOX

## Red Smith's
## Favorite Sports Stories

A *Benjamin Company Book*
IN ASSOCIATION WITH
*Rex Taylor & Company, Inc.*

PUBLISHED BY
*W · W · Norton & Company*
NEW YORK · LONDON

Library of Congress Cataloging in Publication Data
Main entry under title:

Press box: Rex Smith's favorite sports stories.

"A Benjamin Company book in association with Rex Taylor & Company, Inc."
Contents: Graham, F. The best team ever.—Breslin, J. The worst team
ever.—Rice, G. The big fellow.—Heinz, W. C. The ghost of the gridiron [etc.]
1. Sports stories.   I.  Smith, Walter Wellesley, 1905–
GV707.P73   1976        796        75-29404
ISBN 0-393-31002-7

Printed in the United States of America

W. W. Norton & Company, Inc.
500 Fifth Avenue, New York, N.Y. 10110
W. W. Norton & Company Ltd.
10 Coptic Street, London WC1A 1PU

1  2  3  4  5  6  7  8  9

# Contents

# Acknowledgments

"The Best Team Ever," from *The New York Yankees,* by Frank Graham, published by G. P. Putnam's Sons; copyright 1943 by Frank Graham. Reprinted by permission of Mrs. Frank Graham.

"The Worst Team Ever," by Jimmy Breslin, published by *Sports Illustrated;* copyright 1962 by Jimmy Breslin. Reprinted by permission of Jimmy Breslin.

"The Big Fellow," from *The Tumult and the Shouting,* by Grantland Rice, published by A. S. Barnes & Company; copyright 1954 by Grantland Rice. Reprinted by permission of A. S. Barnes & Company.

"The Ghost of the Gridiron," by W. C. Heinz, published by Fawcett Publications, Inc., in *True* magazine; copyright 1958 by W. C. Heinz. Reprinted by permission of W. C. Heinz.

"Dempsey vs. Carpentier," by Irvin S. Cobb, published by the New York *Times* and copyrighted in 1921 by the Central Press Association.

"Hub Fans Bid Kid Adieu," by John Updike, originally published by *The New Yorker* in 1960; copyright 1960 by John Updike. Reprinted by permission of Alfred A. Knopf, Inc.

"The Long Count," by Gene Tunney, published originally by *Field and Stream,* and copyrighted by *Field and Stream.* Reprinted by permission of *Field and Stream.*

"Knute Rockne, the Man and the Legend," by Jack Newcombe, published in 1953 by Macfadden Publications, Inc., in *Sport* magazine; copyright 1953 by Jack Newcombe. Reprinted by permission of Jack Newcombe.

"Louis Knocks Out Schmeling," by Bob Considine, published by International News Service and copyrighted in 1938 by the

Hearst Corporation. Reprinted by permission of the Hearst Corporation.

"The Haig," by John Lardner, published by Fawcett Publications, Inc., in *True* magazine; copyright 1959 by Mrs. John Lardner. Reprinted by permission of Susan Lardner Hellerman.

"A Room at the Barn," by John McNulty, published by *The New Yorker;* copyright 1953 by John McNulty. Reprinted by permission of Faith McNulty.

"Team Bobbing," by Edward J. Neil, published in 1932 by the Associated Press; copyright 1932 by the Associated Press. Reprinted by permission of the Associated Press.

"My Favorite Caddie," from *Thirty Years of Championship Golf,* by Gene Sarazen with Herbert Warren Wind, published by Prentice-Hall, Inc.; copyright 1950 by Prentice-Hall, Inc. Reprinted by permission of Prentice-Hall, Inc.

"Stymie—Common Folks," by Joe H. Palmer, from *This Was Racing,* by Joe H. Palmer, published by Henry Clay Press, 1973. Reprinted by permission.

"The Greatest Tennis Player of All Time," by Allison Danzig, published by the New York *Times;* copyright 1963 by the New York *Times.* Reprinted by permission of the New York *Times.*

"The Iceman Cometh," by Stan Fischler, published by *Sports Illustrated* under the title "A Rough Time on the Road"; copyright 1964 by Time, Inc. Reprinted by permission of *Sports Illustrated.*

"Antonino the Great," by Robert O'Brien, published by *Esquire* magazine; copyright 1959 by Esquire, Inc. Reprinted by permission of *Esquire.*

"Bradley's Last Game for Princeton," from *A Sense of Where You Are,* by John McPhee, published by Farrar, Straus & Giroux; copyright 1965 by John McPhee. Reprinted by permission of Farrar, Straus & Giroux.

# Foreword

## Red Smith

Anyone who sets out to write about sportswriting in America—and it is surprising how many do—inevitably chooses between two positions.

He may subscribe to the view that "some of the best writing in our newspapers appears on the sports pages." (I'm blessed if I can remember who said that first.) Or he may agree with Lewis Gannett, the widely respected book reviewer for the late New York *Herald Tribune*, who wrote:

"For the most part, I think that sports writing is over-praised. American highbrows tend to suffer from inferiority complexes; they yearn to be good lowbrows, too, and claim to find wonderful folk-poetry in comic strips and sports pages. Most comic strips, I think, are dithering nonsense, and most sports writers suffer from hyperthyroid congestion of adjectives and are dope fiends for forced similes. They try to be jitterbugs with words and have no change of pace. They stutter in their excitement."

Both of these positions can be supported. Trouble is, those who adopt the first usually go plunging exuberantly ahead until they seem to be insisting that *all* the best writing in newspapers appears on the sports pages or, even more recklessly, that all writing on the sports pages is good. Those who start from Mr. Gannett's stance seldom resist the temptation to deride all sportswriting as the

product of a sweaty literati whose members find it difficult to read
without facial contortions.

The truth, as usual, lies between the two extremes. Some of the
best writing in our newspapers does appear on the sports pages,
along with some of the worst. Some sportswriters do dither and
stutter; some treat the mother tongue with the respect it deserves.

As a matter of fact, not all sportswriting is done by sportswriters.
Homer, Hazlitt, and Victor Hugo wrote of boxing. Thomas Wolfe,
a baseball fan, celebrated the "velvet geometry of the playing
field." And then there was the case of Laurence Stallings.

Mr. Stallings, novelist, journalist, dramatist, and film scenarist,
had been a war correspondent and was fairly famous for his play
about World War I, *What Price Glory?* In 1925, he took an
assignment from the Hearst newspapers to cover a football game
in Philadelphia between the Universities of Pennsylvania and
Illinois. It was the first eastern appearance of a gifted halfback
named Harold ("Red") Grange.

On a field greasy with mud, Grange ran loose for three touchdowns and raced fifty-five yards to set up another. When it was
over and the sweaty literati were beating out their stuttering
prose, the man who had covered a war was pacing the press box
and clutching his haircut. "I can't!" Stallings was wailing. "I can't
write it! It's too big!"

It is not to be inferred that good sportswriting can be produced
only by people employed in the sports department of a newspaper. One of the finest pieces in this book is John Updike's report
on the last game that Ted Williams played for the Boston Red Sox
in Fenway Park. To the best of my knowledge, John Updike has
never held a card of membership in the Baseball Writers Association of America, but in this piece he does something that no
member of the Association ever did. He tells us why Ted Williams
could not bring himself to acknowledge applause by tipping his
cap like other ballplayers.

"Gods," Updike explains, "do not answer letters."

The amused perception of Irvin S. Cobb at Boyle's Thirty Acres in Jersey City is a delight, and the meticulous profile of Red Grange by W. C. Heinz is a triumph. Frank Graham's low-keyed appraisal of the Yankees of 1927, John Lardner's appreciation of the grandeur that was Hagen, John McPhee's sensitive portrait of Bill Bradley on the basketball court—maybe there are finer examples of clean-limbed English prose, but there aren't many.

The compilation offered here is presented with no boasts that can't be supported. This book is not put forward as the greatest this or the finest that. Readers will find here neither folk poetry nor tone poems, neither ambrosia for the intellectuals nor porridge for the lowbrows—only a few evenings of pure pleasure.

# PRESS BOX

# The Best Team Ever

## *Frank Graham*

Most of us seem to agree that the 1927 New York Yankees, with Babe Ruth, Lou Gehrig, Bob Meusel, and Tony Lazzeri doing the hitting and Waite Hoyt, Herb Pennock, Urban Shocker, George Pipgras, and Wilcy Moore throwing the pitches, was probably the greatest baseball team ever assembled—even better than the Yankees of the late 1930s or the Yankees of the early 1950s. Nobody knew those greatest Yankees better than Frank Graham, who traveled with them and seldom missed a game in the Stadium when he was covering baseball for the old New York *Sun*. Here are his reminiscences of their 1927 season, written for his informal history, *The New York Yankees*, one of the best books in the literature of baseball.

The defeat in the 1926 World Series was a dark interlude between the Yankees' unexpected triumph in the pennant race that year and their rise in 1927 to a peak which many believe they never have surpassed. This, they say, was the team. Greater than any that had gone before, greater than any that has followed.

With few changes, the makeup of the team was the same as 1926: Ruth, Combs, and Meusel in the outfield; Gehrig, Lazzeri, Koenig, and Dugan in the infield. Johnny Grabowski, a good journeyman catcher, had been purchased from the White Sox to work with Bengough and Collins. Cedric Durst and Benny Paschal were the extra outfielders. For protection in the infield, there were Mike Gazella, Roy Morehart, and Julian Wera. The brunt of the pitching would be borne by Hoyt, Pennock, Shocker, and Pipgras, who had been brought back from St. Paul, where he had finished his schooling for the majors. To help out there were Reuther, Thomas, Braxton, Shawkey, and Joe Giard. And to the staff had been added one of the most amazing players ever to wear a Yankee uniform.

His name was Wilcy Moore, and he was a dirt farmer from Hollis, Oklahoma. Nobody knew exactly how old he was. He said he was twenty-eight, but nobody believed him. The chances are he was at least thirty. He was big, broad-shouldered, slow-moving, good-natured, and a great favorite with the other players. For six years he had toiled in the minor leagues with no thought or hope of getting to the majors. He had good years and bad ones. When he picked up a little money, he went home and put it in the bank or bought new tools for his farm.

So far as he was concerned, the 1926 season had been just about the same as other good ones he had had. Pitching for Greenville in the South Atlantic League, he had won thirty games and lost only four. When it ended, he packed his stuff and said good-bye to the other players. Good-bye forever, he thought to himself, for he had about made up his mind that the time had come for him to quit trouping around the country and stay in his fields. And then, the night before he was to leave, he learned that he had been sold to the Yankees.

"I didn't know anybody from the Yankees had looked at me," he said later. "I didn't know they'd ever heard of me. And nobody in our front office ever had said anything to me about me being sold. Maybe it just happened—or maybe they were keeping it as a surprise for me. Anyway, I thought I'd come up and see what it was like up here."

His equipment for pitching in the major leagues was limited but sound. It consisted of a sinker—a low, fast ball that broke sharply downward as it reached the plate—almost flawless control, and nerves of steel—or no nerves at all. He also had, or thought he had, a curve ball, and he used to beg Huggins to let him throw it once in a while, but Hug always shook him off.

"Your curve ball," Hug said, "wouldn't go around a button on my vest."

He was used almost exclusively as a relief pitcher. By common consent of those who played with him or against him, he was the best they ever saw.

The other players, admiring him for his pitching, laughed at him as a hitter. And with reason. He had the perfect stance at the plate and the perfect swing. The only trouble was that he always swung in the same spot, no matter where the ball was, so that if he hit it, it was by accident. Ruth, after one look at him in batting practice at the training camp, bet him $300 to $100 that he wouldn't make three hits all season. He made five. When he got home he wrote the Babe a letter.

"The $300 come in handy," it said. "I used it to buy a fine pair of mules. I named one Babe and the other Ruth."

Once the season opened, there never was any doubt that the Yankees would win the pennant. Ruth, Meusel, Gehrig, and Lazzeri daily terrorized the opposing pitchers, and there wasn't a man in the batting order, down to the pitcher's spot, who couldn't break up a ball game by hitting one out of the park. Hoyt's arm, which had bothered him the year before, was strong again. Pennock was—well, Pennock. Shocker, with proper rest, was a hard man to beat, although by now he was pitching mostly with his head. Huggins picked assignments carefully for Pipgras, and the youngster won regularly. Braxton, Thomas, and the others filled in effectively. When any of the pitchers faltered, there was always Moore. The power of the team blinded the onlookers to the skill and smoothness of its fielding.

Enemy teams cracked and broke wide open before their assaults. When one of them did strike back and put a Yankee pitcher to rout, Moore ambled in from the bullpen, and the struggle was over. There was an incident one night in Detroit when Mike Gazella said something that indicated how the rest of the Yankees felt about Moore. The players were watching a big fire in an office building near their hotel. Flames roared and dense black smoke poured from the stricken building as the constantly augmented ranks of firemen poured water on it from every angle. At last the flames died down and thin white smoke rose from the seared walls.

"We can go home now," Mike said. "They got Wilcy Moore in."

The race virtually was decided as early as the Fourth of July. The Senators, in a June spurt, had moved up on them, and the holiday doubleheader between the teams packed the Stadium. But when the games were over, the departing crowd knew that never again would the Senators be dangerous. The Senators knew it, too; for the Yankees had won the first game 12 to 1 and the second 21 to 1.

Ruth, with his genius for rising to every occasion, was having his greatest season. When he had hit fifty-nine home runs in 1921, it had seemed that no one, himself included, ever would approach that mark. Now he was slamming the ball out of every park on the circuit, and his total was mounting. Gehrig wasn't far behind him. They were the Home Run Twins, Babe and Lou. The greatest combination of power hitters the game had ever known.

The team struck so often in the late innings that Combs called this delayed attack "five o'clock lightning." The phrase caught on, spread through the league and seeped into the consciousness of opposing pitchers. They began to dread the approach of five o'clock and the eighth inning.

Always in demand for exhibition games in the minor league towns during the season since Ruth had been a member of the team, the Yankees were in even greater demand now, so that they scarcely had a day off. Open dates found them in St. Paul, Dayton, Buffalo, Indianapolis. Even Cincinnati and Pittsburgh, having no American League teams, booked them.

Sometimes the players grumbled about this, but actually they enjoyed it. And no one enjoyed it more than the Babe. He snarled traffic and jammed the parks wherever he went. His progress through the countryside was like that of a president or a king. Even in the smallest towns, no matter how late the hour, there would be crowds at the station hoping to catch a glimpse of him. And the Babe never failed them. He would leave his dinner or a card game, even get up out of bed, to go out on the platform and greet his admirers and shake the hands stretched up to him.

"How did you know he was coming through?" a reporter asked a grinning section hand at one crossroads village where, for some reason, the train had stopped one night.

"The station agent told us," he said. "Every station along the line knows he's coming."

One of the secrets of the Babe's greatness was that he never lost any of his enthusiasm for playing ball, and especially for hitting home runs. To him a homer was a homer, whether he hit it in a regular game, a World Series game, or an exhibition game. The crack of his bat, the sight of the ball soaring against the sky—these thrilled him as much as they did the fans.

In Indianapolis one day—this was when the ball park was down by the railroad tracks—he went to bat three times without hitting a ball out of the infield, and the overflow crowd was having a fine time razzing him. But on his fourth trip, he really got hold of one. He hit it high and far over the right-field fence where, as those in the press box on the roof of the grandstand could see, it went bouncing and rolling among the boxcars in the freight yard. The crowd howled. They had seen many a home run, but never one like that. And the Babe? He was as happy as though the world championship had hung on that drive.

"I guess I didn't show those people something!" he said, on his return to the dugout. "Make fun of me, will they?"

In Toronto—the Babe usually played first base, with Gehrig in right field in these games—a crowd of small boys piled down out of the bleachers in the eighth inning, crowded around the big guy, and refused to be driven back by the umpires or even the police. Seeing the situation was hopeless, the umpires called the game, whereupon the kids leaped on the Babe joyfully and bore him to the ground.

"I had the presence of mind," the Babe said, "to put my cap between my teeth and hold onto it like a dog. Otherwise, one of those little suckers would have stole it for a souvenir."

Once the Yankees went to Sing Sing to play the prison team.

The Babe hit one over the right-field wall in batting practice, then hit one over in center, where the yard is deepest. The prisoners roared.

"Well," one of them yelled, "there's something goes out of here anyway!" And another: "Oh, boy! I'd like to be riding on that one!"

The Babe had a great time. When a convict umpire called one of the prison players safe in a close play at the plate, he boomed: "Robber!"

When the Yankees, clowning, permitted a prison player to steal a base, Ruth wanted to know if there weren't any cops in the joint. Turning to the first-base bleachers, he asked what time it was, and when a half dozen inmates eagerly told him, he roared:

"What difference does it make to you guys? You ain't going any place."

The prisoners thought that was wonderful, although if someone else had said it they might have felt differently.

But those were diversions. The serious business of clinching the pennant remained—although it must be said for them that the Yankees attacked that with as much relish as they put into the fun-making. The decisive game took place in Boston on Labor Day. Up to that time they had, for the most part, strictly adhered to the training rules. But that night the lid was off. All Huggins asked them to do was to show up at the Back Bay station in time to get the 1 A.M. train for New York, and they all made it.

There were some passengers on the train who will never forget that they rode with the Yankees that night. The three cars for the players were at the head end of the train, which was unusual. The players clambered aboard near the rear end and marched through. Two of the cars through which they had to pass were compartment cars, and the shoes of the occupant had been placed in front of each closed door for the porter to shine. Someone kicked one of the shoes. The others thought it was a great idea. When the Yankees had passed, there in the forward end of each car was a pile of shoes that must have taken hours to sort the next morning.

Having clinched the pennant, the Yanks kept right on hammering. They wanted to win—and did—every game they possibly could. They set an American League record which still stands by winning 110 games and losing 44. They won the pennant by seventeen games. Ruth smashed his own record for home runs by hitting sixty and had a batting average of .356. Gehrig hit .373 and made forty-seven homers. Hoyt, with twenty-two victories, was the league's leading pitcher in games won and lost. Moore, with an average of 2.28 was the best in the matter of earned runs allowed.

In the National League the Pittsburgh Pirates, under Donie Bush, had won the pennant after a terrific struggle with the Cardinals. This was a good team, with Clyde Barnhart and the Waner brothers, Lloyd and Paul, in the outfield, Joe Harris at first base, George Grantham at second, Glenn Wright at shortstop, the great Pie Traynor at third base, Earl Smith and Johnny Gooch to divide the catching, and such pitchers as Ray Kramer, Vic Aldrich, Lee Meadows, Carmen Hill, and Johnny Miljus.

The Series opened in Pittsburgh. Hotel accommodations were inadequate for the crowds that poured into the town. For a while, nobody seemed to know where the Yankees could be housed. Just in time Barrow received word that a new hotel, the Roosevelt, had been completed and would throw open its doors to the Yankees as its first guests. On the bulletin board in the club house at the Stadium the day the team left New York was a notice:

"The Yankees will open the Hotel Roosevelt in Pittsburgh."

And under it a player wrote, in pencil:

"And how!"

All was confusion in the hotel when they arrived early in the morning of the day before the first game. The lobby was packed with fans eager for a close-up of Ruth, Gehrig, Lazzeri, Pennock, and the other famous players—so packed that Huggins, his short-stemmed pipe in his mouth and his dinky traveling bag in one hand—almost was trampled in the rush as the players made their way to the desk.

Arrangements had been made for the Pirates to work out about ten o'clock that morning and then withdraw, leaving the field to the Yankees. By the time the Yankees appeared, the Pirates had dressed and were in the stands. Also in the stands or hovering back of the plate were the newspapermen and photographers sent from all over the country to cover the Series.

"You're starting tomorrow, Waite," Huggins said to Hoyt. "Go out there and take about ten minutes of batting practice. Just lay the ball in there."

Straight as a string, Hoyt laid the ball up to the plate. Combs, Koenig, Ruth, Gehrig, Meusel, Lazzeri, Dugan, Collins, Grabowski walked up and hit it. Up against the stands. Into the stands. Over the fences. It was a terrifying demonstration of power hitting.

In the stands the Waner brothers, great ballplayers in their own right but little men, stood talking with Ken Smith, New York *Mirror* reporter, as the Yankees slugged the ball. Ruth hit one over the fence in center field, Gehrig hit one high in the seats in right field. Meusel hit one over the fence in left field. Lloyd turned to Paul.

"Jesus," he said fervently. "They're big guys!"

Paul shook his head. The Waners walked out. Most of their teammates followed them. They had seen enough. It is undoubtedly true that right there the Yankees won the Series. Before a ball had been pitched in actual competition, they had convinced the Pirates that theirs was a losing cause.

The Yankees won the first game, 5 to 4, with Hoyt taking a decision over Kramer. Hoyt failed to finish the game, however. He got in trouble in the eighth inning and was hauled out, whereupon Moore stalked in from the bullpen to turn the Pirates back and sew up the game.

Pipgras hooked up with Aldridge in the second game, and the Yankees romped in, 6 to 2. There were some who thought Huggins was taking a long chance in starting Pipgras, but the youngster vindicated his manager's judgment by yielding only seven hits scattered over as many innings.

Now the Series moved to New York. As the Yankees were riding down to the station that night, a newspaperman in a cab with Lazzeri and three other players said:

"If you fellows don't wind this Series up in these next two games, I'll shoot you."

And Lazzeri said: "If we don't beat these bums four in a row, you can shoot me first."

The other players nodded. That's the way everybody on the ball club felt.

Huggins called on Pennock in the opening game in New York, defying the dope that no left-hander could beat the Pirates. For seven innings, pitching against Meadows, Pennock did not allow a hit and, the way he was going, it looked as though he would be the first pitcher in World Series history to hang up a no-hit game. Ironically, he was stalled by his own teammates, for in the eighth inning the Yankees, runless since the first, when they had scored twice, set upon Meadows savagely, drove him from the box, and scored six runs, one of which was a homer by Ruth. Sitting on the bench through that long half inning, Pennock cooled out. He got rid of Wright, the first man to face him in the eighth, but Traynor singled and Barnhart doubled, Traynor scoring. In the ninth Lloyd Waner singled to left. Pennock had missed a no-hit game and a shutout as well. But his three-hit performance, the score of which was 8 to 1, still stands as one of the finest ever seen in a World Series.

Later, in the club house, the taciturn Meusel was moved to ask: "Who said a left-hander couldn't beat the Pirates?"

And a reporter, to whom the question was addressed, said:

"Plenty of guys. But they meant the left-handers in the National League. They haven't any like Pennock in that league."

The outcome of the Series now was assured. The Yankees not only would win but would win in four games, as they had promised themselves. They did it, too. But not without a few chills and shakes along the way. The Pirates, probably reckoning that all was lost anyway, were free of the tension which had gripped them through the three preceding games and put up a stubborn struggle against Moore, who was allowed to pitch a game of his own as a reward for his great relief work during the season. Ruth, who had driven in the Yankees' first run in the first inning, made his second homer of the Series off Hill in the fifth with Combs on base. But the Pirates, who also had made a run in the first, made two in the seventh, and the game went into the last half of the ninth still tied.

Hill had been removed for a pinch hitter in the seventh, and Miljus was pitching for the Pirates. He walked Combs, leading off, and Koenig, intending only to sacrifice, beat out the bunt he had rolled toward third base. With Ruth up, Miljus let go with a wild pitch and the runners moved up. Miljus then purposely passed the Babe and the bases were filled. With Gehrig and Meusel coming up, Miljus really was in a jam; but, pitching desperately, he fanned both. There still was Lazzeri. In his eagerness to get rid of Tony, Miljus turned on too much stuff. A fast ball, sailing, whizzed over Gooch's head as the catcher tried frantically to knock it down, and Combs crossed the plate with the winning run.

Colonel Jacob Ruppert, the owner of the Yankees, trembling in his box next to the dugout as the struggle went on, was almost incoherent with joy as he saw Combs racing home and realized that once more his team was the best in the world.

# The Worst
# Team Ever
## Jimmy Breslin

If the 1927 New York Yankees were the best team ever, which one was the worst in the history of major-league baseball? Everybody gives that award to the New York Mets of 1962, managed by the same Casey Stengel who previously directed the Yankees to ten pennants and seven World Series championships, which only goes to show that a baseball team needs more than a manager. Jimmy Breslin was so fascinated by those Mets that he wrote a book about them entitled *Can't Anybody Here Play This Game?* Later, when Marvin Throneberry, the worst Met, was finally traded to Buffalo, Breslin reported that Marv was unable to open the door of Stengel's office in order to hear that sad news. "He kept turning the doorknob the wrong way," Breslin said. "Gil Hodges had to open the door for him."

It was long after midnight. The bartender was falling asleep and the only sound in the hotel was the whine of a vacuum cleaner in the lobby. Casey Stengel banged his last empty glass of the evening on the red-tiled bar top and then walked out of this place the Chase Hotel in St. Louis calls the Lido Room.

In the lobby the guy working the vacuum cleaner was on his big job, the rug leading into the ballroom, when Mr. Stengel stopped to light a cigarette and reflect on life. For Stengel this summer, life consists of managing a team called the New York Mets, which is not very good at playing baseball.

"I'm shell-shocked," Casey said to the cleaner. "I'm not used to getting any of these shocks, and now they come every three innings. How do you like that?" The cleaner had no answer. "This is a disaster," Casey continued. "Do you know who my player of the year is? My player of the year is Choo Choo Coleman and I have him for only two days. He runs very good."

This accomplished, Stengel headed for bed. The cleaner went back to his rug. He was a bit puzzled, although not as much as Stengel was later in the day when the Mets played the St. Louis Cardinals in a doubleheader.

Casey was standing on the top step of the dugout at Busch Stadium and he could see the whole thing clearly. That was the trouble.

In front of him the Mets had Ken Boyer of the Cardinals in a rundown between first and second. Marvin Throneberry, the marvelous first baseman, had the ball. Boyer started to run away from him. Nobody runs away from Marvin Throneberry. He took after Boyer with a purpose. Marv lowered his head a little and produced wonderful running action with his legs. This amazed Stengel. It also amazed Stan Musial of the Cardinals, who was on third. Stanley's mouth opened. Then he broke for the plate and ran across it and into the dugout with the run that cost the Mets the game. (Throneberry, incidentally, never did get Boyer. Charlie Neal finally made the putout.) It was an incredible play. It was also loss No. 75 of the season for the Mets. In the second game, Roger Craig, the Mets' starting pitcher, gave up so many runs so quickly in the seventh inning that Casey didn't have time to get one of his great relief pitchers ready. The Mets went on to lose No. 76.

Following this the team flew to New York, where some highly disloyal people were starting to talk about them. There seems to be some sort of suspicion around that the New York Mets are not only playing baseball poorly this summer but are playing it worse than any team in the modern history of the sport. As this week began, the Mets had a record of 28 wins and 79 losses and seemed certain to break the record for losses in one season. This was set by the 1916 Philadelphia Athletics, who lost 117 games, an achievement that was challenged by the Boston Braves of 1935, who lost

115 games and were known as The World's Worst Team. But,
using one of the more expensive Keuffel & Esser slide rules, you
discover that the Mets, if they cling to their present pace, will lose
120 games. You cannot ask for more than that.

Figures, of course, are notorious liars, which is why accountants
have more fun than people think. Therefore, you just do not use a
record book to say the Mets are the worst team of all time. You
have to investigate the matter thoroughly. Then you can say the
Mets are the worst team of all time.

"I never thought I would have an argument," Bill Veeck says. "I
was always secure in the knowledge that when I owned the St.
Louis Browns, I had the worst. Now it's different. You can say
anything you want, but don't you dare say my Brownies were this
bad. I'll prove it to you. There are still a few of those Browns in the
major leagues and this is nine years later. How many Mets do you
think are going to be still around even two years from now? I'm
being soft here. I haven't even mentioned my midget, Eddie
Gaedel."

Reporting from Philadelphia is Pat Hastings, proprietor of the
Brown Jug bar and a man who has sat through more bad baseball
than anybody in America. For consistency, Philadelphia baseball
always has been the worst. In nine years during Pat's tenure at the
old Baker Bowl and Shibe Park, both the Phillies and the A's
finished in last place.

But Pat, who has viewed the Mets on several occasions this
season, refuses to put any team in a class with them. "The 1916
Athletics had Stuffy McInnes, you got to remember that," he says.
"And some of them Phillies teams could hurt you with the bat
pretty good. There was players like Chuck Klein, Virgil Davis,
Don Hurst. I seen 'em all. Why, we used to make jokes about Buzz
Arlett. He played right field for the Phillies in 1931. People used
to go out and get drunk if they seen him catch a fly ball. I feel like
writing the fellow a letter of apology now. Why, he done more
fielding standing still than some of these Mets I seen do at full
speed."

In Brooklyn, there is Joseph (Babe) Hamberger, who once was

associated with the old Dodgers and vehemently denies that he ever saw a Brooklyn club as bad as the Mets.

"When Uncle Robbie [Wilbert Robinson] was managing, he didn't even know the names of the players," Babe says, "but he won two pennants and was in the first division a couple of times. Casey was over here. Ask him. He'll tell you. It got rough, but never like it is with these Mets."

Now all this is not being pointed out as an act of gratuitous cruelty. Quite the opposite. The Mets are so bad you've got to love them. Name one true American who could do anything but root for a team that has had over 135 home runs hit against it. In New York, a lot of people root for the Mets. They are mainly old Brooklyn Dodger fans and their offspring. They are the kind of people who, as Garry Schumacher of the Giants once observed, never would have tolerated Joe DiMaggio on their team in Ebbets Field. "Too perfect," Garry said.

The Mets are bad for many reasons, one of which is that they do not have good players. The team was formed last year when the National League expanded to 10 teams. ("We are damn lucky they didn't expand to 12 teams," Manager Stengel says.) The other new team, the Houston Colt 45s, has done a bit better than the Mets. It is in eighth place, 11½ games ahead of New York. For players, the Mets were given a list of men made available to them by the other eight National League teams. The list was carefully prepared and checked and re-checked by the club owners. This was to make certain that no bona-fide ballplayers were on it.

"It was so thoughtful of them," Stengel says. "I want to thank all of them owners who loved us to have those men and picked them out for us. It was generous of them."

Actually, the Mets did wind up with a ballplayer or two. First Baseman Gil Hodges was fielding as well as ever before a kidney ailment put into the hospital. Center Fielder Richie Ashburn, at 35, is still a fine lead-off hitter, although he seems to be on his way to making some sort of record for being thrown out while trying to take an extra base. If Jim Hickman, an outfielder, ever learns to

swing at good pitches, he might make it big. Here and there, Al
Jackson and Roger Craig produce a well-pitched game. And Frank
Thomas can hit. But all this does is to force the Mets to go out of
their way to lose.

And once past those people named above, the Mets present an
array of talent that is startling. Many of those shocks Casey talks
about come when his pitchers throw to batters. There was a recent
day in St. Louis when Ray Daviault threw a low fast ball to Charley
James of the Cards. James likes low fast balls. He hit this one eight
rows deep into left field for the ball game.

"It was bad luck," Daviault told the manager after the game. "I
threw him a perfect pitch."

"It couldn't have been a perfect pitch," Casey said. "Perfect
pitches don't travel that far."

One of Casey's coaches is the fabled Rogers Hornsby. Rajah was
batting coach during spring training and for the early part of the
season. Now all his work is done with prospects out on the farms.
Which is good because Hornsby hates to lose. One day he was
sitting in the dugout at the Polo Grounds before a game and you
could see him seething. The Mets had been losing. So was
Hornsby. He couldn't get a thing home and he was in action at
three or four different major tracks around the country.

"You can't trust them old Kentucky bastard trainers," he confided.

The general manager of the Mets is George Weiss, who was let
go by the Yankees after the 1960 season because of his age. He is 68
now. George spent all of last year at his home in Greenwich,
Connecticut. As Red Smith reported, this caused his wife, Hazel,
to announce, "I married George for better or for worse, but not for
lunch." She was pleased when George took over the Mets and
resumed his 12-hour working day away from home.

The Mets also have many big-name sports reporters who write
about them. This may be the hardest job of all. As Barney Kre-
menko of the New York *Journal-American* observes, "I've covered losing teams before. But for me to be with a *non-winner!*"

There are some people, of course, who will not stand still for any raps at the team. They say the Mets have a poor record because they lose so many one-run games. They point out that the Mets have lost 28 games by one run so far. However, this figure also indicates that the Mets lost 51 other games by more than one run.

One who advances the one-run theory is Donald Grant, the Wall Street stockbroker who handles ownership details for Mrs. Joan Payson, the class lady who puts up the money for the Mets. It is Mr. Grant's job to write letters to Mrs. Payson, explaining to her what is happening with the Mets.

"It is annoying to lose by one run, but Mrs. Payson and I are pleased with the team's progress," Grant says. "She is perfectly understanding about it. After all, you don't breed a thoroughbred horse overnight." Grant obviously doesn't know much about horse breeding.

The Mets lose at night and lose in the daytime and they lose so much that the only charge you can't make against them is that their pitchers throw spitters.

"Spitters?" Stengel says. "I can't even get them to throw regular legal dry pitches good."

Basically, the trouble with the Mets is the way they play base-ball—walks, passed balls, balks, missed signs, errors, overrun bases and bad throws. You see it every time they play. It doesn't matter if they win or lose. With this team nothing changes. Only the days.

On July 22, for example, the Mets were in Cincinnati for a doubleheader. They not only lost both games, but they also had four runners thrown out at home plate during the course of the day. What made it frightening was the ease with which the Mets brought the feat off. You got the idea that they could get four runners thrown out at the plate any day they wanted to.

In the first game, Choo Choo Coleman was out trying to score from second on a single to left. In the second game Stengel jauntily ordered a double steal in the second inning. He had Cannizzaro on first and Hot Rod Kanehl on third. Cannizzaro took off and drew a throw. Kanehl broke for the plate. The Cincinnati shortstop cut off the throw to second and threw home to take care of Kanehl. In the fourth inning Elio Chacon tried to score from first when the Reds messed up a fly in the outfield. But Vada Pinson finally got to the ball and his throw beat Chacon at the plate by a couple of steps. In the fifth inning, Jim Hickman was on third. He broke for the plate as Rod Kanehl hit the ball. Kanehl's hit went straight to the third baseman, who threw Hickman out by a yard.

The day before that, Roger Craig, the team's big pitcher, had gone to Stengel and volunteered for relief pitching in that day's doubleheader if it was needed. It was nice of Craig to say that he was willing to work between his regular starts. Stengel nodded. And the next day the Mets certainly did need Craig. Going into the ninth inning, tied with the Reds 3–3, Stengel called on Roger to save the day. Roger took his eight warmup pitches. Then he threw two pitches to Marty Keough of the Reds. Keough hit the second pitch eight miles and the Reds won, 4–3.

Two days later in the first inning of a game in Milwaukee, Braves had runners on first and second. Henry Aaron, at bat, hit the ball hard but Chacon at shortstop made a fine backhanded stop. Chacon saw Roy McMillan of the Braves running for third base. Chacon yelled at Felix Mantilla, the Mets' third baseman, to cover that base. He was going to throw out McMillan at third. Mantilla backed up toward third base to take the throw. Then he backed up some more. By the time Chacon threw the ball, Mantilla backed up to a point three yards behind the bag, and when he finally caught the ball, McMillan, standing on third base, was beyond his reach.

The Mets fought back, however, and had the game tied, 4–4 in the twelfth. Casey called on a new pitcher to face the Braves in this inning. He was R. G. Miller, making his first appearance as a Met. At the start of the season, R. G. was managing an automobile sales agency and had no intention of playing baseball. Then Wid Matthews, the Mets' talent scout, came to talk to him. Miller, Matthews found out, needed only 18 days more in the major leagues to qualify as a five-year veteran under the baseball players' pension regulations. R. G. had pitched for Detroit before deciding to sell cars instead.

"Go to Syracuse for us," Matthews said, "and if you show anything at all, we'll bring you up to New York. Then you can put in your 18 days, and when you reach 50, you'll start getting about $125 a month until they put you in a box."

Miller went out front and spoke to his boss. He was told that his job would be waiting for him after the season. So Miller went to Syracuse. He pitched well enough there to be brought up to the Mets. Now he was coming out of the Mets' bullpen to take on the Milwaukee Braves.

Miller loosened up easily, scuffed the dirt, looked down and got the sign and glared at Del Crandall, the Milwaukee batter. Then Miller threw a slider and Crandall hit a home run. Miller, with his first pitch of the season, had lost a game.

"He makes the club," everybody said.

Marvin Throneberry, the fast-running first baseman, has had his share of travail this year, too. In fact, any time you meet an old-timer who tries to bore you with colorful stories, you can shut him up with two Marv Throneberry stories for every one he has about players like Babe Herman or Dizzy Dean.

Throneberry is a balding 28-year-old who comes out of Memphis. He was up with the Yankees, and once even opened a season as a first baseman for them. After that he was with the Kansas City A's and the Orioles. Throneberry is a serious ballplayer. He tries, and he has some ability. It's just that things happen when he plays.

Take the doubleheader against the Cubs at the Polo Grounds early in the season. In the first inning of the first game, Don Landrum of the Cubs was caught in a rundown between first and second. Rundowns are not Throneberry's strong point. In the middle of the posse of Mets chasing Landrum, Throneberry found himself face to face with the Cub runner. The only trouble was that Marvin did not have the ball. During a rundown, the cardinal rule is to get out of the way if you do not have the ball. If you stand on the baseline, the runner will deliberately bang into you, claim interference, and the umpire will give him his claim.

Which is exactly what happened to Marv. Landrum jumped into his arms and the umpire waved Landrum safely back to first base. That opened the gates for a four-run Chicago rally.

Marv had a chance to get even when the Mets came to bat. With two runners on base, Marv drove a long shot to the bullpen in right center field. It looked like a sure triple. Marv flew past first. Well past it. He didn't come within two steps of touching the bag. Then he raced on toward second and careened toward third. While all this violent motion was taking place, Ernie Banks, the Cubs' first baseman, casually strolled over to Umpire Dusty Boggess.

"Didn't touch the bag, you know, Dusty," Banks said. Boggess nodded. Banks then called for the ball. The relay came to him and he stepped on first base. Across the infield Throneberry was standing on third, proudly hitching up his belt, when he saw the umpire calling him out at first.

Marv has been rankled only once all year. He was irked by Ed Bouchee who replaced him at first base in a couple of games. In San Francisco one day, Roger Craig, who has a fine pickoff motion for a righthander, fired the ball to first and had Orlando Cepeda of the Giants clearly nailed. But Bouchee dropped the throw. Two windups later, Craig again fired the ball to first. He had Cepeda off the bag, leaning toward second. It was an easy pickoff. The ball again bounded out of Bouchee's glove.

Back in New York, when Bouchee appeared on the field at the Polo Grounds, the fans gave him a good going-over.

"What are you trying to do?" Throneberry complained to Bouchee. "Steal my fans?"

It has been a rough season for Mr. Stengel but he is standing up under the strain and trying. After one long afternoon, he was asked about a couple of particularly costly misplays by Throneberry and Charlie Neal.

"Ah!" Casey said. "Bonehead. They was bonehead plays. Damn bonehead plays!" His eyes flashed. Then he leaned back, quieted down and spoke in a soft voice. "Look," he said. "I can't change a man's life. I got four or five guys who are going to make it up here. The rest of them, we just got to get along with. I'm not goin' to start breaking furniture because of them. It's the man, and I got him and I can't change his life."

Then he got dressed and a man named Freddie picked up his suitcase and led him out of the dressing room. They had a taxicab waiting across the street, in front of an old, one-story brick-front place named Marge's Tavern. Casey pushed through the crowd and got into the taxi. He was carrying on a running conversation with the crowd as he shut the door and the taxi started to pull away.

It was, you figured, the way it should be. For over 50 years now, Casey Stengel has been getting into taxis in front of old saloons across the street from a ball park. He has done this with great teams and with bad teams. Now he has the worst outfit anybody ever saw. But even if the players don't belong, Stengel does. He'll be back next year.

God help him.

# The Big Fellow

## Grantland Rice

Grantland Rice and Babe Ruth, close friends, were also both the friendliest and best-liked champions in the realm of sports. An incurable romantic, Granny gave his heroes such poetic titles as "The Manassa Mauler" and "The Galloping Ghost," and it was he who first hailed the 1924 Notre Dame backfield as "The Four Horsemen." As he recalls in this tribute to the most popular athletic hero in American sports history, Babe Ruth was a fellow who said exactly what he was thinking. During one springtime salary dispute, the Babe was reminded that he was demanding more money than Herbert Hoover had received the previous year for being President of the United States. "Why not?" Ruth said. "I had a better year than Hoover."

The first time I saw Babe Ruth was in April, 1919, when he was taking his turn in batting practice at the spring training camp of the Boston Red Sox at Tampa, Florida. Since covering my first World Series in 1905, I had seen a lot of swingers but never a swinger like this one.

Babe blasted one pitch out of the park, into a ploughed field. I gauged that as about 500 feet, and while Ruth went on hitting I talked with Ed Barrow, the Red Sox manager. "He's been signed to a three year contract," Barrow said. "At twenty four, this fellow can be the greatest thing that's happened to baseball. He's a fine southpaw pitcher—he can become a great one. But the day when I can use him in the outfield and take advantage of his bat every day—well, they'll have to build parks bigger, just for Ruth."

After bombing about ten shots, Ruth circled the bases, with short, pigeon-toed steps, a base-circling trot destined to become as celebrated as Man o' War's gallop. When Ruth came to the bench to mop his face with a towel, Barrow introduced us.

"You sound like you got a cold," said Ruth.

"I have, sort of," I said.

Taking an enormous red onion out of his hip pocket, Ruth thrust it into my hand. "Here," he said, "gnaw on this. Raw onions are cold killers." While Ruth talked, I gnawed, with tears streaming from my eyes.

From the start, Ruth and I hit it off. An absolutely honest man, the Babe said exactly what he thought. The Chicago White Sox, he said that day, had a smart, hustling team, and Boston would need the breaks to stick close to them.

"Babe," I said, "I was watching your swing. You swing like no pitcher I ever saw."

"I may be a pitcher, but first off I'm a hitter," said Babe. "I copied my swing after Joe Jackson's. His swing is the perfectest. Joe aims his right shoulder square at the pitcher, with his feet about twenty inches apart. But I closed my stance to about eight and a half inches, or less. I find I can pivot better with it closed. Once my swing starts, I can't change it or pull up on it. It's all or nothing at all."

Throughout his career of twenty years, Ruth never changed the basics of that gorgeous, gargantuan arc—a swing that fascinated the crowd as much as the personality of the man behind it. To watch Ruth go down swinging, often sprawling from the violence of his cut, was almost as exciting as seeing him blast one out of the park.

Of all the sluggers spawned by the advent of the lively baseball in the 1920s, Babe was the only one who never choked or shortened his grip when two strikes were called against him. He gripped his bat with the knob of the handle palmed in his right hand. So perfectly timed was his swing and his wrist-snap that he could wait on the pitch, watching it until the last split second, and "pick" the ball when it was practically in the catcher's mitt. Ted Williams was the only other long ball hitter with this amazing faculty of judging a pitch until the very last moment before deciding whether or not to swing at it.

The Babe liked plenty of lumber in his war clubs. Many of them were about a half-pound heavier than the average bat.

That spring the Red Sox and John McGraw's Giants played a four-out-of-seven game exhibition series at Tampa. The New York writers were pop-eyed over Ruth's hitting. In the first game, he drove the longest ball we ever saw over the right center field fence. Bill McGeehan of the New York *Tribune*, who wasn't impressed easily, wrote, "The ball sailed so high that it came down coated with ice—a drive that would have rattled off the clubhouse roof at the Polo Grounds."

That series with the Giants put an exclamation mark on Ruth, the hitter, and wrote finis on his pitching career. That was O.K. with Babe. Ruth, as an outfielder, would no longer have to muscle his way into batting practice.

"I came up as a southpaw pitcher," he said later, "and pitchers aren't supposed to clutter up the batter's box trying to hit during batting practice. I saw no reason why I shouldn't get my licks. I got them usually but there were times when I'd go to my locker next day and find my bats sawed in half."

Boston finished in sixth place at the end of that 1919 season as Chicago's brilliant team roared to the pennant, despite Ruth's 29 homers. In January, 1920, when Harry Frazee, the owner of the Red Sox, was trying to get out of debt, he sold Ruth to Jake Ruppert's third place New York Yankees for $125,000, plus a loan of $350,000. The transaction was baseball's all-time bargain. The Chicago Black Sox scandal—the throwing of the 1919 World Series by eight Chicago players—was revealed and investigated during the 1920 season, when Ruth was making his debut in New York. Baseball sorely needed a new superstar to restore public trust in the game, and Babe Ruth was the savior. The game's leaders moved to help him by giving the ball a shot of rabbit juice to make it livelier. Seeing the ball being smashed out of the park more frequently would remove any doubts about the authenticity of the scores. In 1920, Babe boomed 54 homers, changing the style of the game, introducing the big scoring inning. That season, playing their home games in the Giants' Polo Grounds while the new Yankee Stadium was being built on the opposite side of the Harlem River, the Yankees drew bigger crowds than the Giants. In 1921, 1922, and 1923, the Yanks and the Giants met in the World Series, 1923 being the first year that the Series was played in Yankee Stadium, "The House That Ruth Built." Some baseball writers claimed that the short right field fence in the new stadium was deliberately designed for Ruth's left-handed hitting. But there was nothing questionable about a home run that Ruth hit in the Yankees' first game at the Stadium on April 18, 1923, to beat the Red Sox, 4 to 1, before the largest crowd in the history of baseball up to that time. Heywood Broun, who covered the game for the New York *World,* wrote, "It would have been a home run in the Sahara Desert."

Ruth seldom mentioned his childhood. Actually, I think that it had been so miserable that he had put it out of his memory and could recall little of it. He was in Saint Mary's Industrial Home in Baltimore, an institution for wayward boys, from the age of eight until he was seventeen. Then Brother Gilbert, the headmaster of the home, turned him over to the custody of Jack Dunn, the manager of the Baltimore Orioles, then a baseball club in the minor International League. Dunn signed him for the 1914 season for $600. Johnny Evers, the keystone of the famous Tinker-to-Evers-to-Chance double play combination, once passed on to me an account of how Ruth's father had committed him to the industrial home, which, Johnny said, the Babe had told him.

Ruth said he had taken a dollar from his family's till and had bought ice cream cones with it for all of the kids on his block. "When my old man asked me what I did with the dollar, I told him," the Babe told Evers. "He dragged me down to the cellar and horsewhipped me. I tapped the till again, just to show him he couldn't break me. Then I landed in the home, thank God."

Tom Meany, writing a book about the Babe's life, ran into a tout at a New York racetrack, a seller of printed tip sheets, who said that he had spent his childhood with the Babe at "The Home." "You know, either Babe's gone soft or I've gone nuts," the tout told Tom. "But I hafta laugh when I hear that place mentioned as 'The Home.' There was guys with guns on the walls."

Small wonder that after such a childhood Babe Ruth's life as a baseball hero seemed like Christmas every day in the year.

The Babe was a big and often losing gambler. In less than two weeks at Charles Stoneham's Oriental Park racetrack in Havana in the winter of 1925, he lost between thirty and fifty thousand dollars. That cured him of betting on the horses. He became interested in college football but he wagered on only one game, as far as I know. "I bet five thousand on them Harvards," he told me one time, "but the Yales win it. I'm off that football business, too."

In March of 1933, when I was heading south for the spring training season, I stopped in Georgia at the shooting preserve of Bob Woodruff, the Coca-Cola king. When it came time for me to move on to Florida, Woodruff gave me his car and chauffeur and a luggage compartment loaded with game birds. "I'll throw a Florida dinner in your honor," I said to him. "We'll feast on Woodruff's eighteen-carat birds, basted with Coca-Cola."

"If you do," Woodruff said, "I wish you'd invite Walter Lippmann and his wife. They're down near Bradenton, and they're good friends of mine."

The dinner, to which Babe was also invited, was a huge success until the dignified Mrs. Lippmann asked Babe to describe the home run that he "called" in the 1932 World Series against the Cubs, a four-straight rout for the Yankees.

"It's like this," boomed the Babe, bigger than a freshly laundered barn in his white gabardine suit, and puffing on a huge cigar. "The Cubs had (censored) my old teammate, Mark Koenig, by cutting him in for a measley, (censored) half-share of their Series money. Well, I'm riding the (censored) out of the Cubs, telling 'em they're the cheapest pack of (censored) crumbums in the world. We win the first two and now we're in Chicago for the third

game. Root is the Cubs' pitcher. I pack one into the stands in the
first inning off him, but in the fifth it's tied four to four when I'm up
with nobody on. The Cub fans are giving me hell. Root's still in
there. He freezes the first two pitches by me—both strikes. After
the second strike, I point my bat at those bellering bleachers, right
where I aim to park the ball. Root throws it, and I hit that
(censored) ball on the nose—right over the (censored) fence for
another (censored) run. 'How do you like those apples, you (censored, censored, censored),' I yell at Root as I head towards first.
By the time I reach home, I'm almost falling down I'm laughing so
(censored) hard—and that's how it happened."

After the Babe's baccalaureate finished, a battered Mrs. Lippmann mumbled that perhaps she and her husband had better be
leaving. A minute later the Walter Lippmanns were history.

"Why did you use that language?" I asked Babe.

"What the hell, Grant," he said. "You heard her ask me what
happened. So I told her."

As a golfer, Ruth was a long but not terrific hitter. I was with him
at Clearwater, Florida, when he was betting Babe Didrikson that
he could outdrive her tee shots, $50 a drive. She outdrove Ruth by
at least 20 yards for $200 before he was convinced. But nobody
ever enjoyed the game, or cussed it and his playing, more than
Ruth. One morning in 1933 Babe and I had a date to play with
Dizzy Dean at Clearwater. Having only recently taken up the
game, Diz was pretty wild with his woods and long irons. "I got a
bushel of bets riding with Dean today," bellowed Ruth. "I'm
giving him strokes on ten different holes and I'm going to collect
on all of 'em."

When we reached the club, Babe spotted Pat Dean, Dizzy's
handsome bride, who had driven her husband to the course.

"Pat," said Babe, "come on out with us this morning. The walk
will do you good."

Babe's invitation puzzled Pat but she accepted it. Diz said
nothing. After one sloppy shot by Diz on the second hole, Pat
commented, "Dear, you're ducking."

Dean exploded.

"Ducking, hell!" he roared at his wife. "Who invited you on this rabbit shoot anyhow?"

Ruth howled with laughter. Pat stalked off in a rage. Dean couldn't hit a shot for the rest of the round. The Babe never collected an easier hatful.

When the Yankees were heading north from spring training in 1934, Babe's last year with the club, he developed at Atlanta a sudden huge hankering for chicken Georgia style. I called Bob Woodruff and mentioned Babe's craving for local chicken. "I'll send my car over," Bob said, naming several places to get chicken. "Take it and look over these spots." Bob Jones added a few more suggestions. Clare Ruth, Babe and I inspected the places on the list and ultimately selected a small hideaway restaurant several miles from town. The proprietor promised to prepare four of Georgia's finest hens for a dinner that would be served to us after that day's exhibition game. As we were leaving, Babe admired the spring flowers on the front lawn. He plucked one and handed it to Clare.

"They're pretty daisies," he remarked.

"No, dear, they're daffodils," Mrs. Ruth said.

"They're still daisies to me," Babe said. Any flower, from a dandelion to a white orchid, was a daisy to him.

Ruth went to the showers that day after the sixth inning. Then we returned to our hacienda dining room, where the proprietor was beaming when he greeted us. He was flanked by a retinue of popeyed excited waiters.

"The chickens, they are prepared," said our host proudly.

"Chickens hell!" Ruth roared. "I want beef steak!"

He got it. The next day he visited his Georgian friend, Bob Jones, the great golfer. We were fanning highballs in Bob's living room when Bob Jones III, then a youngster, roared into the house with all of the kids in the neighborhood. "That's *him!*" Bobby cried. If Santa Claus had visited 32–50 Northside Drive that afternoon, he would have been ignored. Babe grabbed an old bat from one of the kids, found it was cracked, and tore it apart.

"Bobby, make your old man buy you a *good* bat," Babe said.

Babe sincerely loved kids because in many ways he was a big kid himself. I went to his room for dinner on the eve of the World Series in Chicago in 1932. He always ate in his hotel room on the road because in the dining room downstairs he would have been mobbed by fans and autograph hunters.

"I've got to go out on a short trip, Grant," he said.

"Where are you going on the night before a World Series?"

"I'll tell you, but if you print it, I'll shoot you. I'm going to take a baseball to a sick kid on the other side of town. I promised his mother and father. He's pretty sick."

The house was twenty or thirty miles away, over an hour to get there and another hour to get back. No publicity.

Babe was personally acquainted with more policemen than any athlete who ever lived. The motorcycle cops enjoyed escorting him to Yankee Stadium or helping him to get away from the crowd after a game. They were usually there, like the Travelers' Aid, when Babe needed a safe trip home to his apartment on Riverside Drive after a late party.

One morning Babe called me and asked for a ride to our planned golf game at Leewood in Tuckahoe. "Sure," I said, "but what happened to your car?"

"I lost it," he said.

"Lost it? You had it last night."

"That was last night," Babe said. "I wrecked it somewhere in Westchester and left it there." So he had. The cops had driven him home. One day, at a Babe Ruth Day festival in the Stadium, he was presented with a new Stutz roadster. An hour later, in the parking lot behind the nearby Grand Concourse Hotel, he turned the car over. Another time when Babe was roaring along a highway in the dawn's early light, he was stopped by a policeman who suggested that he was in no condition to drive.

"Why you (censored)!" Babe roared, and punched the cop.

"Now I *know* you're drunk," the cop said. "Move over. I'm driving you home."

Another evening he was stopped while driving the wrong way on a one-way street.

"I'm only driving one way!" Ruth yelled at the policeman.

"Oh, hello, Babe," the cop said. "I didn't know it was you. Go anywhere you like, but take it easy."

I was once on a national radio broadcast with Babe and Graham McNamee. He was to read a prepared script, carefully timed. He rehearsed it and had it down practically letter-perfect. But then when we went on the air after the big musical introduction, everything went to pieces. Before I could throw a halter on the Babe, he was off and running. McNamee was frantic, the orchestra leader was frantic, the producer was frantic, but Ruth rambled on. At one point, the Babe was supposed to refer to the Duke of Wellington's historic remark that the Battle of Waterloo had been won on the playing fields of Eton.

"As Duke Ellington said," the Babe proclaimed, "the Battle of Waterloo was won on the playing fields of Elkton."

Later I asked Babe how he managed to louse up that one short statement so completely.

"About the Wellington guy, I wouldn't know," he said. "Ellington, yes. As for the Eton business, well, I married my first wife in Elkton, Maryland, and I always hated the goddamned place. It musta stuck in my mind."

One evening Babe and I were having a few drinks in the grill room of the Chatham Hotel. Suddenly he looked at his watch and cried, "Jesus! I gotta run!" In a flash he was grabbing his hat and coat and flagging a cab. Alarmed, I asked what the trouble was.

"Trouble?" Ruth yelled. "Why, 'Gangbusters' is on the radio!"

Ruth loved crowds and the crowds always came to see him hit. He was the greatest magnet that sport has ever known. Jack Dempsey was another big gate attraction, but he defended his heavyweight title only four times in seven years. Babe played every day, six months of the year, for nearly fifteen years and he packed the stands in every big city and in bush league exhibitions. He seldom missed a curtain call. I have traveled all over the map with him, and whenever the train stopped at a station, or the car pulled up to a hotel, a crowd gathered around him, waving to him and calling his name.

"How can they miss this silly mug?" he would say.

He always enjoyed living, and he was always kindly to every-body—so kindly. There was the big day when Marshal Foch, the French commander of the Allied forces in World War I, came to see a game of American baseball at Yankee Stadium. The Babe was introduced to the great hero, and after they shook hands, there was a pause while Ruth tried to think of something friendly to say, something to make the distinguished visitor feel at ease. Babe studied his own shoes for a moment. Then he looked up at the celebrated soldier and smiled at him.

"You were in the war, weren't you?" Babe said pleasantly.

# The Ghost of
# the Gridiron
## W. C. Heinz

Harold Edward Grange of the University of Illinois and the
Chicago Bears was probably the greatest broken-field runner in
the history of football and, along with Babe Ruth and Jack
Dempsey, one of the most famous athletes of the 1920s, the
so-called Golden Age of Sports. This profile of Red Grange by
W. C. Heinz, one of the most talented sportswriters of our time,
was published in 1958, when Grange was fifty-five years old and
living in semi-retirement in Florida. Bill Heinz never saw
Grange play football, except in the movies, but his portrait of the
Galloping Ghost is by far the best one that anybody has ever
written.

When I was ten years old I paid ten cents to see Red Grange run
with a football. That was the year when, one afternoon a week,
after school was out for the day, they used to show us movies in the
auditorium, and we would all troop up there clutching our dimes,
nickels or pennies in our fists.

The movies were, I suppose, carefully selected for their educa-
tional value. They must have shown us, as the weeks went by,
films of the Everglades, of Yosemite, of the Gettysburg battle-
field, of Washington, D.C., but I remember only the one about
Grange.

I remember, in fact, only one shot. Grange, the football cradled
in one arm, started down the field toward us. As we sat there in the
dim, flickering light of the movie projector, he grew larger and

larger. I can still see the rows and rows of us, with our thin little necks and bony heads, all looking up at the screen and Grange, enormous now, rushing right at us, and I shall never forget it. That was thirty-three years ago.

"I haven't any idea what film that might have been," Grange was saying now. "My last year at Illinois was all confusion. I had no privacy. Newsreel men were staying at the fraternity house for two or three days at a time."

He paused. The thought of it seemed to bring pain to his face, even at this late date.

"I wasn't able to study or anything," he said. "I thought and I still do, that they built me up out of all proportion."

Red Grange was the most sensational, the most publicized, and, possibly, the most gifted football player and greatest broken field runner of all time. In high school, at Wheaton, Illinois, he averaged five touchdowns a game. In twenty games for the University of Illinois, he scored thirty-one touchdowns and ran for 3,637 yards, or, as it was translated at the time, 2 miles and 117 yards. His name and his pseudonyms—The Galloping Ghost and The Wheaton Iceman—became household words, and what he was may have been summarized best by Paul Sann in his book *The Lawless Decade*.

"Red Grange, No. 77, made Jack Dempsey move over," Sann wrote. "He put college football ahead of boxing as the Golden Age picked up momentum. He also made the ball yards obsolete; they couldn't handle the crowds. He made people buy more radios: how could you wait until Sunday morning to find out what deeds Red Grange had performed on Saturday? He was 'The Galloping Ghost' and he made the sports historians torture their portables without mercy."

Grange is now 55 years old, his reddish brown hair marked with gray, but he was one with Babe Ruth, Jack Dempsey, Bobby Jones and Bill Tilden.

"I could carry a football well," Grange was saying now, "but I've met hundreds of people who could do their thing better than I. I mean engineers, and writers, scientists, doctors—whatever.

"I can't take much credit for what I did, running with a football, because I don't know what I did. Nobody ever taught me, and I can't teach anybody. You can teach a man how to block or tackle or kick or pass. The ability to run with a ball is something you have or you haven't. If you can't explain it, how can you take credit for it?"

This was last year, and we were sitting in a restaurant in Syracuse, New York. Grange was in town to do a telecast with Lindsey Nelson of the Syracuse–Penn State game. He lives now in Miami, Florida, coming out of there on weekends during the football season to handle telecasts of college games on Saturdays and the Chicago Bears' games on Sundays. He approaches this job as he has approached every job, with honesty and dedication, and, as could be expected, he is good at it. As befits a man who put the pro game on the map and made the whole nation football conscious, he has been making fans out of people who never followed the game before. Never, perhaps, has any one man done more for the game. And it, of course, has been good to him.

"Football did everything for me," he was saying now, "but what people don't understand is that it hasn't been my whole life. When I was a freshman at Illinois, I wasn't even going to go out for football. My fraternity brothers made me do it."

He was three times All-American. Once the Illinois students carried him two miles on their backs. A football jersey, with the number 77 that he made famous and that was retired after him, is enshrined at Champaign. His fellow students wanted him to run for Congress. A Senator from Illinois led him into the White House to shake hands with Calvin Coolidge. Here, in its entirety, is what was said.

"Howdy," Coolidge said. "Where do you live?"

"In Wheaton, Illinois," Grange said.

"Well, young man," Coolidge said, "I wish you luck."

Grange had his luck, but it was coming to him because he did more to popularize professional football than any other player before or since. In his first three years out of school he grossed almost $1,000,000 from football, motion pictures, vaudeville appearances and endorsements, and he could afford to turn down a Florida real estate firm that wanted to pay him $120,000 a year. Seven years ago the Associated Press, in selecting an All-Time All-American team in conjunction with the National Football Hall of Fame, polled one hundred leading sportswriters and Grange received more votes than any other player.

"They talk about the runs I made," he was saying, "but I can't tell you one thing I did on any run. That's the truth. During the depression, though, I took a licking. Finally I got into the insurance business. I almost starved to death for three years, but I never once tried to use my football reputation. I never once opened a University of Illinois year book and knowingly called on an alumnus. I think I was as good an insurance man as there was in Chicago. On the football field I had ten other men blocking for me, but I'm more proud of what I did in the insurance business, because I did it alone."

Recently I went down to Miami and visited Grange in the white colonial duplex house where he lives with his wife. They met eighteen years ago on a plane, flying between Chicago and Omaha, on which she was a stewardess, and they were married the following year.

"Without sounding like an amateur psychologist," I said, "I believe you derive more satisfaction from what you did in the insurance business, not only because you did it alone, but also because you know how you did it, and, if you had to, you could do it again. You could never find any security in what you did when you ran with a football because it was inspirational and creative, rather than calculated."

"Yes," Grange said, "you could call it that. The sportswriters used to try to explain it, and they used to ask me. I couldn't tell them anything."

I have read what many of those sportswriters wrote, and they had as much trouble trying to corner Grange on paper as his opponents had trying to tackle him on the field. . . .

Grange had blinding speed, amazing lateral mobility, and exceptional change of pace and a powerful straight-arm. He moved with high knee action, but seemed to glide, rather than run, and he was a master at using his blockers. What made him great, however, was his instinctive ability to size up a field and plot a run the way a great general can map not only a battle but a whole campaign.

"The sportswriters wrote that I had peripheral vision," Grange was saying. "I didn't even know what the word meant. I had to look it up. They asked me about my change of pace, and I didn't even know that I ran at different speeds. I had a cross-over step, but I couldn't spin. Some ball carriers can spin but if I ever tried that, I would have broken a leg."

Harold Edward Grange was born on June 13, 1903, in Forksville, Pennsylvania, the third of four children. His mother died when he was five, and his sister Norma died in her teens. The other sister, Mildred, lives in Binghamton, New York. His brother, Garland, two and half years younger than Red, was a 165-pound freshman end at Illinois and was later with the Chicago Bears and is now a credit manager for a Florida department store chain. Their father died at the age of 86.

"My father," Grange said, "was the foreman of three lumber camps near Forksville, and if you had known him, you'd know why I could never get a swelled head. He stood six-one and weighed 210 pounds, and he was quick as a cat. He had three hundred men under him and he had to be able to lick any one of them. One day he had a fight that lasted four hours."

Grange's father, after the death of his wife, moved to Wheaton, Illinois, where he had relatives. Then he sent the two girls back to Pennsylvania to live with their maternal grandparents. With his sons, he moved into a five-room apartment over a store where they took turns cooking and keeping house.

"Can you recall," I said, "the first time you ever ran with a football?"

"I think it started," Grange said, "with a game we used to play without a football. Ten or twelve of us would line up in the street, along one curb. One guy would be in the middle of the road and the rest of us would run across the street to the curb on the other side. When the kid in the middle of the street tackled one of the runners, the one who was tackled had to stay in the middle of the street with the tackler. Finally, all of us, except one last runner, would be in the middle of the street. We only had about thirty yards to maneuver in and dodge the tackler. I got to be pretty good at that. Then somebody got a football and we played games with it on vacant lots."

In high school Grange won sixteen letters in football, basketball, track and baseball. In track he competed in the 100 and 220 yard dashes, low and high hurdles, broad jump and high jump and often won all six events. In his sophomore year on the football team, he scored 15 touchdowns, in his junior year 36—eight in one game—and in his senior year 23. Once he was kicked in the head and was incoherent for 48 hours.

"I went to Illinois," he was saying, "because some of my friends from Wheaton went there and all the kids in the state wanted to play football for Bob Zuppke and because there weren't any athletic scholarships in those days and that was the cheapest place for me to go to. In May of my senior year in high school I was there for the Interscholastic track meet, and I just got through broad jumping when Zup came over. He said, 'Is your name Grainche?' That's the way he always pronounced my name. I said, 'Yes.' He said, 'Where are you going to college?' I said, 'I don't know.' He put his arm around my shoulders and he said, 'I hope here. You may have a chance to make the team here.' That was the greatest moment I'd known."

That September, Grange arrived at Champaign with a battered second-hand trunk, one suit, a couple of pairs of trousers and a sweater. He had been working for four summers on an ice wagon in Wheaton and saving some money, and his one luxury now that he was entering college was to pledge Zeta Phi fraternity.

"One day," he was saying, "they lined us pledges up in the living room of the fraternity house. I had wanted to go out for basketball and track—I thought there would be too much competition in football—but they started to point to each one of us and tell us what to go out for: 'You go out for cheerleader. You go out for football manager. You go out for the band.' When they came to me, they said, 'You go out for football.'

"That afternoon I went over to the gym. I looked out the window at the football practice field and they had about three hundred freshman candidates out there. I went back to the house and I said to one of the seniors, 'I can't go out for football. I'll never make that team.'

"So he lined me up near the wall, with my head down, and he hit me with this paddle. I could show you the dent in that wall where my head took a piece of plaster out—this big."

With the thumb and forefinger of his right hand, he made a circle the size of a half dollar.

"Do you remember the name of that senior?" I said.

"Johnny Hawks," Grange said. "He was from Goshen, Indiana, and I see him now and then. I say to him, 'Damn you. If it wasn't for you, I'd never have gone out for football.' He gets a great boot out of that."

"So what happened when you went out the next day?"

"We had all these athletes from Chicago I'd been reading about. What chance did I have, from a little farm town and a high school with three hundred students? I think they cut about forty that first night, but I happened to win the wind sprints and that got them at least to know my name."

It was a great freshman team. On it with Grange was Earl Britton, who blocked for Grange and did the kicking throughout their college careers, and Moon Baker and Frank Wickhorst, who transferred to Northwestern and Annapolis, respectively, where they both made All-America. After one week of practice, the freshman team played the varsity and were barely nosed out, 21–19, as Grange scored two touchdowns, one on a 60 yard punt return. From then on, the freshmen trimmed the varsity regularly and Zuppke began to give most of his time to the freshmen.

"That number 77," I said to Grange, "became the most famous number in football. Do you remember when you first got it?"

"It was just handed to me in my sophomore year," he said. "I guess anybody who has a number and does well with it gets a little superstitious about it, and I guess that began against Nebraska in my first varsity game."

That game started Grange to national fame. This was 1923, and the previous year Nebraska had beaten Notre Dame and they were to beat "The Four Horsemen" later this same season. In the first quarter Grange sprinted 35 yards for a touchdown. In the second quarter he ran 60 yards for another. In the third period he scored again on a 12 yard burst, and Illinois won, 24–7. The next day, over Walter Eckersall's story in the Chicago *Tribune*, the headline said: GRANGE SPRINTS TO FAME.

From the Nebraska game, Illinois went on to an undefeated season. Against Butler, Grange scored twice. Against Iowa, he scored the only touchdown as Illinois won, 9–6. In the first quarter against Northwestern, he intercepted a pass and ran 90 yards to score the first of his three touchdowns. He made the only touchdown in the game with the University of Chicago and the only one in the Ohio State game, this time on a 34 yard run.

"All Grange can do is run," Fielding Yost, the coach at Michigan, was quoted as saying.

"All Galli-Curci can do is sing," Zuppke said.

Grange had his greatest day in his first game against Michigan during his junior year. On that day Michigan came to the dedication of the new $1,700,000 Illinois Memorial Stadium. The Wolverines had been undefeated in twenty games and for months the nation's football fans had been waiting for this meeting. There were 67,000 spectators in the stands, then the largest crowd ever to see a football game in the Midwest.

Michigan kicked off. Grange was standing on his goal line, with Wally McIlwain, whom Zuppke was to call "the greatest open field

blocker of all time" on his right, Harry Hall, the Illinois quarterback, on his left, and Earl Britton in front of him. Michigan
attempted to aim the kickoff to McIlwain, but as the ball descended, Grange moved over under it.

"I've got it," he said to McIlwain.

He caught it on the 5 yard line, McIlwain turned and took out
the first Michigan man to get near him. Britton cut down the next
one, and Grange started underway. He ran to his left, reversed his
field to avoid one would-be tackler, and, then, cutting back again
to the left, ran diagonally across the field through the oncoming
Michigan players. At the Michigan 40 yard line he was in the open
and on the 20 yard line, Tod Rockwell, the Michigan safety man,
made a futile dive for him. Grange scored standing up. Michigan
never recovered.

In less than twelve minutes, Grange scored three more touchdowns on runs of 67, 56 and 44 yards. Zuppke took him out to rest
him. In the third period, he re-entered the game, and circled right
end for 15 yards and another touchdown. In the final quarter, he
threw a pass for another score. Illinois won, 39–14. Against a
powerful, seasoned and favored team, Grange had handled the
ball twenty-one times, gained 402 yards running, scored five
touchdowns and collaborated, as a passer, in a sixth.

"This was," Coach Amos Alonzo Stagg, the famous Chicago
mentor, later wrote, "the most spectacular singlehanded performance ever made in a major game."

"Did Zuppke tell you that you should have scored another
touchdown?" I asked Grange.

"That's right," Grange said. "After the fourth touchdown we
called a time-out, and when Matt Bullock, our trainer, came with
the water, I said to him, 'I'm dog tired. You'd better tell Zup to get
me out of here.' When I got to the bench Zup said to me, 'You
should have had five touchdowns. You didn't cut right on one
play.' Nobody could get a swelled head around him."

"And you don't recall," I said, "one feint or cut that you made
during any one of those runs?"

"I don't remember one thing I ever did on any run I made. I just remember one vision from that Michigan game. On that opening kick-off runback, as I got downfield I saw that the only man still in front of me was the safety man, Tod Rockwell. I remember thinking then, 'I'd better get by this guy, because after coming all this way, I'll sure look like a bum if he tackles me.' I can't tell you, though, how I did get by him."

When Grange started his senior year, Illinois had lost seven regulars by graduation and Harry Hall, its quarterback, who had a broken collarbone. Zuppke shifted Grange to quarterback. Illinois lost to Nebraska, Iowa and Michigan and barely beat Butler before they came to Franklin Field in Philadelphia on October 31, 1925, to play Pennsylvania.

The previous year Penn had been considered the champion of the East. They had now beaten Brown, Yale and Chicago, among others. Although Grange's exploits in the Midwest had been widely reported in Eastern papers, most of the 65,000 spectators and the Eastern sportswriters—Grantland Rice, Damon Runyon and Ford Frick among them—came to be convinced.

It had rained and snowed for 24 hours, with only straw covering the field. At the kickoff, the players stood in mud. On the third play of the game, the first time he carried the ball, Grange went 55 yards for his first touchdown. On the next kickoff he ran 55 yards again, to the Penn 25 yard line, and Illinois worked it over the goal line from there. In the second period, Grange twisted 12 yards for another score and in the third period he ran 20 yards to a touchdown. Illinois won, 24–2, with Grange carrying the ball 363 yards, and scoring three touchdowns and setting up another one, in thirty-six rushes.

Two days later when the train carrying the Illinois team arrived in Champaign, there were 20,000 students, faculty members and townspeople waiting at the station. Grange tried to sneak out of the last car but he was recognized and carried two miles to his fraternity house.

"Do you remember your feelings during those two miles?" I asked him.

"I remember that I was embarrassed," he said. "You wish people would understand that it takes eleven men to make a football team. Unless they've played it, I guess they'll never understand it, but I've never been impressed by individual performances in football, my own or anyone else's."

"Do you remember the last touchdown you scored in college?"

"To tell you the truth, I don't," he said. "It must have been against Ohio State. I can't tell you the score. I can't tell you the score of more than three or four games I ever played in."

I looked it up. Grange's last college appearance, against Ohio State, attracted 85,500 spectators at Columbus. He was held to 153 yards on the ground but threw one touchdown pass as Illinois won, 14–9. The following afternoon, in the Morrison Hotel in Chicago, he signed with Charles C. (Cash and Carry) Pyle to play professional football with the Chicago Bears, starting immediately, and he quit college. Twenty-five years later, however, he was elected to the University of Illinois Board of Trustees for a six-year term.

"I had a half year to finish when I quit," he said. "I had this chance to make a lot of money and I couldn't figure where having a sheepskin would pull any more people into football games."

"How were your marks in college?"

"I was an average student. I got B's and C's. I flunked one course, economics, and I made that up in the summer at Wheaton College. I'd leave the ice wagon at 11 o'clock in the morning and come back to it at 1 o'clock. There was so much written about my job on the ice wagon, and so many pictures of me lugging ice, that people thought it was a publicity stunt. It wasn't. I did it for eight summers, starting at 5 o'clock every morning, for two reasons. The pay was good—$37.50 a week—and I needed money. I didn't even have any decent clothes until my junior year. Also, it kept me in shape. After carrying those blocks of ice up and down stairs six days a week, my legs were always in shape when the football season started. Too many football players have to play their legs into shape in the first four or five games."

Grange played professional football from 1925 through the 1934 season, first with the Bears, then with the New York Yankees in a rival pro league that Pyle and he started, and then back with the Bears again. He was immobilized during the 1928 season with arm and knee injuries, and after that he was never able to cut sharply while carrying the ball. He did, however, score 162 touchdowns as a professional and kicked 86 conversion points, for a total of 1,058 points.

What the statistics do not show, however, is what Grange, more than any other player, did to focus public attention and approval on the professional game. In 1925, when he signed with the Bears, professional football attracted little notice on the sports pages and few paying customers. There was so little interest that the National Professional Football League did not even hold a championship playoff at the end of the season.

In ten days after he left college Grange played five games as a pro and changed all that. After only three practice sessions with the Bears, he made his pro debut against the Chicago Cardinals on Thanksgiving Day, November 26. The game ended 0–0 but 36,000 people crowded into Wrigley Field to see Grange. Three days later, on a Sunday, 28,000 defied a snowstorm to watch him perform at the same field. On the next Wednesday, freezing weather in St. Louis held the attendance down to 8,000 but on Saturday 40,000 Philadelphians watched him in the rain at Shibe Park. The next day the Bears played in the Polo Grounds against the New York Giants.

It had been raining for almost a week, and, although advance sales were almost unknown in pro football in those days, the Giants sold almost 60,000 before Sunday dawned. It turned out to be a beautiful day. Cautious fans who had not bought seats in advance stormed the ticket booths. Thousands of people were turned away but 73,651 crammed into the park. Grange did not score but the Bears won, 19–7.

That was the beginning of professional football's rise to its present popularity. At the end of those first ten days, Grange picked up a check for $50,000. He got another $50,000 when the season ended a month later.

"Can you remember," I asked him now, "the last time you ever carried a football?"

"It was in a game against the Giants in Gilmore Stadium in Hollywood in January of 1935. It was the last period, and we had a safe lead and I was sitting on the bench. George Halas said to me, 'Would you like to go in, Red?' I said, 'No, thanks.' Everybody knew this was my last year. He said, 'Go ahead. Why don't you run it just once more?'

"So I went in, and we lined up and they called a play for me. As soon as I got the ball and started to go I knew that they had it framed with the Giants to let me run. The line just opened up for me and I went through and started down the field. The farther I ran, the heavier my legs got and the farther those goal posts seemed to move away. I was thinking, 'When I make that end zone, I'm going to take off these shoes and shoulder pads for the last time.' With that something hit me from behind and down I went on about the 10 yard line. It was Cecil Irvin, a 230-pound tackle. He was so slow that, I guess, they never bothered to let him in on the plan. But when he caught me from behind, I knew I was finished."

Grange, who is 5 feet 11 and ¾ inches, weighed 180 in college and 185 in his last game with the Bears. Now he weighs 200. On December 15, 1951, he suffered a heart attack. This motivated him to give up his insurance business and to move to Florida where he and his wife own, in addition to their own home in Miami, land in Orlando and Melbourne and property at Indian Lake.

"Red," I said, "I'll bet there are some men still around whose greatest claim to fame is that they played football with you or against you. I imagine there are guys whose proudest boast is that they once tackled you. Have you ever run into a guy who thought he knew everything about football and didn't know he was talking with Red Grange?"

"Yes," he said. "Once about fifteen years ago, on my way home from work, I dropped into a tavern in Chicago for a beer. Two guys next to me and the bartender were arguing about Bronco Nagurski and Carl Brumbaugh. On the Bears, of course, I played in the backfield with both of them. One guy doesn't like Nagurski and he's talking against him. I happen to think Nagurski was the greatest football player I ever saw, and a wonderful guy. This fellow who is knocking him says to me, 'Do you know anything about football? Did you ever see Nagurski play?' I said, 'Yes, and I think he was great.' The guy gets mad and says, 'What was so great about him? What do you know about it?' I could see it was time to leave, but the guy kept at me. He said, 'Now wait a minute. What makes you think you know something about it? Who are you, anyway?' I reached into my wallet and took out my business card and handed it to him and started for the door. When I got to the door, I looked back at him. You should have seen his face."

Mrs. Grange, who had been listening to our talk, left the room and came back with a small, gold-plated medal that Grange had won in the broad jump at the Interscholastic track meet on the day when he first met Zuppke.

"A friend of mine just sent that to me," Grange said. "He wrote: 'You gave me this away back in 1921. I thought you might want it.' Just the other day I got a letter from a man in the Midwest who told me that his son just found a gold football inscribed, 'University of Illinois, 1924' with the initials H. G. on it. I was the only H. G. on that squad so it must have been mine. I guess I gave it to somebody and he lost it. I wrote the man back and said: 'If your son would like it, I'd be happy to have him keep it.' "

Mrs. Grange said, "We have a friend who can't understand why Red doesn't keep his souvenirs. He has his trophies in another friend's storage locker in Chicago. The clipping books are nailed up in a box in the garage here and Red hasn't looked at them in years."

"I don't like to look back," Grange said. "You have to look ahead."

I remembered that night when we ate in the restaurant in Syracuse. As we stood in line to get our hats and coats, Grange nudged me and showed me his hat check. In the middle of the yellow cardboard disk was the number 77.

"Has this ever happened to you before?" I said.

"Never," he said, "as far as I know."

We walked out into the cold night air. A few flakes of snow were falling.

"That jersey with the 77 on it that's preserved at Illinois," I said, "is that your last game jersey?"

"I don't know," Grange said. "It was probably a new jersey."

"Do you have any piece of equipment that you wore on the football field?"

"No," he said. "I don't have anything."

The traffic light changed, and we started across the street. "I don't even have an I-sweater," he said.

We walked about three paces.

"You know," Grange said, "I'd kind of like to have an I-sweater now."

# Dempsey vs. Carpentier

## Irvin S. Cobb

Not only the sports section, but almost the whole issue of the New York *Times* on Sunday, July 3, 1921, including Page One and the news pages that followed it, was filled with headlines, stories, and pictures of the previous afternoon's heavyweight championship fight between Jack Dempsey and Georges Carpentier at Boyle's Thirty Acres in New Jersey. No other sports event, before or since, was ever given such coverage. Prominently displayed on the front page of the *Times* and running over on most of page 9 was Irvin S. Cobb's lengthy and colorful report on the scene and the action, written at the ringside before and during the fight, each page telegraphed to the office in New York as it came out of his typewriter. Here is on-the-spot reporting at its classic best.

Through a hundred entrances the multitude flows in steadily, smoothly, without jamming or confusion. The trickling streams run down the aisles and are absorbed by capillary attraction in the seats. If it takes all sorts of people to make up the world then all the world must be here already. That modest hero of the cinema, Tom Mix, known among friends as the Shrinking Violet of Death Valley, starts a furor by his appearance at 12:15, just as the first of the preliminary bouts is getting under way. His dress proclaims that he recently suffered a personal bereavement. He is in mourning. He wears a sea-green sport suit, a purple handkerchief, a pair of solid-gold filled glasses and a cowboy hat the size of a six-furlong track. Actress ladies in make-up and also some few in citizens' clothes jostle against society leaders and those who follow in their wake.

The arts, the sciences, the drama, commerce, politics, the bench, the bar, the great newly risen bootlegging industry—all these have sent their pink, their pick and their perfection to grace this great occasion. A calling over of the names of the occupants of the more highly priced reservations would sound like reading the first hundred pages of Who's Ballyhoo in America. Far away and high up behind them, their figures cutting the skyline of the mighty wooden bowl, are perched the pedestrian classes. They are on the outer edge of events if not actually in it.

Conspicuous at the front, where the lumber-made cliffs of the structure shoal off into broad flats, is that type which is commonest of all alongside a fight ring. He is here in numbers amounting to a host. There must be thousands of him present. He is the soft-fleshed, hard-faced person who keeps his own pelt safe from bruises, but whose eyes glisten and whose hackles lift at the prospect of seeing somebody else whipped to a soufflé. He is the one who, when his favorite pug is being hammered to a sanguinary Spanish omelet, calls out: "That's all right, kid, he can't hurt you." I see him countlessly repeated. For the anonymous youths who in the overtures are achieving a still greater namelessness by being put violently to sleep he has a listless eye. But wait until the big doings start. Then will his gills pant up and down as his vicarious lusting for blood and brute violence is satisfied.

Bout after bout is staged, is fought out, is finished. Few know who the fighters are and nobody particularly cares. Who is interested in flea-biting contests when he came to see a combat between young bull elephants? Joe Humphries, the human Cave of the Winds, bulks as a greater figure of interest as he vouches for the proper identities of these mute, inglorious preliminary scrappers than do the scrappers themselves.

It's one o'clock now. Where an hour ago there were wide vacant stretches of unoccupied seating space, now all is covered with piebald masses—the white of straw hats, the black of men's coats, with here and there bright patches of cola-like peonies blossoming in a hanging garden, to denote the presence of many women in gay summer garb. The inflowing tides of humanity have inundated and swallowed up the desert. Still there has been no congestion, no traffic jams. However the fight may turn out, the handling of the crowd has been competent. Tex Rickard is the world's greatest showman.

The hour of one has arrived. Harry Stevens, the official caterer, can't figure within ten thousand of what the full attendance will be and so prepares to slice another ham. One thing is sure—today Boyle's Thirty Acres has given to Tex Rickard a richer harvest than any like area of this world's surface ever yielded.

At this moment—one-sixteen—atmospheric troubles impend. A drizzle has begun to fall. It is a trickle as yet but threatens to develop into an authentic downpour. The air has grown sodden and soggy with moisture thickened to the saturation point. It is as though one breathed into a wet sponge. I figure this sort of thing, continuing or growing worse, will slow up the two chief clouters when their turn comes.

Governor Edwards of New Jersey comes at one-thirty: the first good solid knock-down in the ring at one-thirty-six. Both are heartily approved with loud thunders of applause. Not everyone can be the anti-dry sport-loving governor of a great commonwealth, but a veritable nobody can win popular approval on a day like this by shoving his jaw in front of a winged fist. There are short cuts to fame though painful.

The shower has suspended, but the atmosphere is still as soppy as a wet shirt. This certainly is a stylish affair. I have just taken note of the fact that the corps of referees all wear white silk blouses and white trousers like tennis players and that the little fat boy who holds up big printed cards with numerals on them to show the number of the next round is done up in spotless white linen like an antiseptically bandaged thumb. The humidity with which the air is freighted is beginning now to be oppressive. Even the exertion of shoving a pencil across paper brings out the perspiration and the two ambitious novices up in the ring are so wet and so slick with their own sweat that they make you think of a pair of fresh-caught fish flapping about in a new sort of square net.

It's three o'clock. Prompt on the appointed hour, for once in the history of championship goes, the men are brought forth on time. Carpentier comes first, slim, boyish, a trifle pale and drawn-looking, to my way of thinking. He looks more like a college athlete than a professional bruiser. A brass band plays the "Marseillaise," men and women stand to greet him—or maybe the better to see him—and he gets a tremendous heartening ovation. Dempsey follows within two minutes. A mighty roar salutes him, too, as he climbs into the ring and seats himself within the arc of a huge floral horseshoe; but so near as may be judged by the applause for him, an American born, it is not so sincere or spontaneous as the applause which has been visited upon the Frenchman.

He grins—but it is a scowling, forbidding grin—while photographers flock into the ring to focus their boxes first on one and then on the other. Dempsey sitting there makes me think of a smoke-stained Japanese war idol; Carpentier, by contrast, suggests an Olympian runner carved out of fine grained white ivory. Partisans howl their approval of the champion. He refuses to acknowledge these. One figures that he has suddenly grown sulky because his reception was no greater than it was.

A little crowd of ring officials surround Dempsey. There is some dispute seemingly over the tapes in which his knobby brown hands are wrapped. Carpentier, except for one solicitous fellow-countryman, is left quite alone in his corner.

Dempsey keeps his eyes fixed on his fists. Carpentier studies him closely across the eighteen feet which separates them. The Gaul is losing his nervous air. He is living proof to give the lie to the old fable that all Frenchmen are excitable.

Overhead aeroplanes are breezing, and their droning notes come down to be smitten and flung up again on the crest of the vast upheaval of sound rising from the earth. A tiresome detail of utterly useless announcements is ended at last.

As the fighters are introduced, Dempsey makes a begrudged bow, but Carpentier, standing up, is given such an ovation as never before an alien fighter received on American soil. It is more plain by this test who is the sentimental favorite. The bettors may favor Jack; the populace likes Georges.

Without handshaking they spring together; Carpentier lands the first blow. Dempsey, plainly enraged, is fast; Carpentier is faster still. But his blows seem to be wild, misplaced, while Dempsey, in the clinches into which they promptly fall, plans punishing licks with swift, short-armed strokes. The first half minute tells me the story. The Frenchman is going to be licked, I think, and that without loss of time. A tremendous roar goes up as Dempsey brings the first blood with a glancing lick on the side of his opponent's nose; it increases as the Frenchman is shoved half through the ropes. The first round is Dempsey's all the way. He has flung Carpentier aside with thrusts of his shoulders. He has shoved him about almost at will.

But midway of the second round Carpentier shows a flash of the wonderful speed for which he is known. With the speed he couples an unsuspected power. He is not fighting the defensive run-away-and-come-again fight that was expected of him. He stands toe to toe with Dempsey and trades 'em. He shakes Dempsey with a volley of terrific right-handed clouts which fall with such speed you do not see them. You only see that they have landed and that Dempsey is bordering on the state technically known as groggy.

It is a wonderful recovery for the Frenchman. His admirers shriek to him to put Dempsey out. To my mind the second round is his by a good margin. Given more weight I am sure now that he would win. Yet I still feel sure Dempsey's superiority in gross tonnage and his greater aptitude at in-fighting will wear the lesser man down and make him lose.

The third round is Dempsey's from bell to bell. He makes pulp of one of Carpentier's smooth cheeks. He pounds him on the silken skin over his heart. He makes a xylophone of the challenger's short ribs. The Frenchman circles and swoops, but the drubbing he gets makes him uncertain in his swings. Most of his blows go astray. They fly over Dempsey's hunched shoulders—they spend themselves in the air.

In the fourth round, after one minute and sixteen seconds of hard fighting—fighting which on Carpentier's part is defensive —comes the foreordained and predestined finishment. I see a quick flashing of naked bodies writhing in and out, joining and separating. I hear the flop, flap, flop of leather bruising human flesh. Carpentier is almost spent—that much is plain to every one. A great spasmodic sound—part gasp of anticipation, part groan of dismay, part outcry of exultation—rises from a hundred thousand throats. Carpentier totters out of a clinch; his face is all spotted with small red clots. He lunges into the air, then slips away, retreating before Dempsey's onslaught, trying to recover by foot-work. Dempsey walks into him almost deliberately, like a man aiming to finish a hard job of work in workmanlike shape. His right arm crooks up and is like a scimitar. His right fist falls on the Frenchman's exposed swollen jaw; falls again in the same place even as Carpentier is sliding down alongside the ropes. Now the Frenchman is lying on his side.

Dempsey knows the contract is finished—or as good as finished. Almost nonchalantly he waits with his legs spraddled and his elbows akimbo harkening to the referee's counting. At the toll of eight Carpentier is struggling to his knees, beaten, but with the instinct of a gallant fighting man, refusing to acknowledge it. At nine he is up on the legs which almost refuse to support him. On his twisted face is the look of a sleep-walker.

It is the rule of the ring that not even a somnambulist may be spared the finishing stroke. Thumbs down means the killing blow, and the thumbs are all down for the stranger.

For the hundredth part of a second—one of those flashes of time in which an event is photographed upon the memory to stay there forever, as though printed in indelible colors—I see the French-man staggering, slipping, sliding forward to his fate. His face is toward me and I am aware at once his face has no vestige of conscious intent. Then the image of him is blotted out by the intervening bulk of the winner. Dempsey's right arm swings upward with the flailing emphasis of an oak cudgel and the muffled fist at the end of it lands again on its favorite target—the Frenchman's jaw.

The thud of its landing can be heard above the hysterical shrieking of the host. The Frenchman seems to shrink in for a good six inches. It is as though that crushing impact had telescoped him. He folds up into a pitiable meager compass and goes down heavily and again lies on the floor, upon his right side, his face half covered by his arms as though even in the stupor following that deadly collision between his face and Dempsey's fist, he would protect his vulnerable parts. From where I sit writing this I can see one of his eyes and his mouth. The eye is blinking weakly, the mouth is gaping, and the lips work as though he chewed a most bitter mouthful. I do not think he is entirely unconscious; he is only utterly helpless. His legs kick out like the legs of a cramped swimmer. Once he lifts himself half-way to his haunches. But the effort is his last. He has flattened down again and still the referee has only progressed in his fateful sum of simple addition as far as "six."

My gaze shifts to Dempsey. He has moved over into Carpentier's corner and stands there, his arms extended on the ropes in a posture of resting. He has no doubt of the outcome. He scarcely shifts his position while the count goes on. I have never seen a prizefighter in the moment of triumph behave so. But his expression proves that he is merely waiting. His lips lift in a snarl until all his teeth show. Whether this be a token of contempt for the hostile majority in the crowd, or merely his way of expressing to himself his satisfaction is not for me to say.

The picture lingers in my mind after the act itself is ended. Behind Dempsey is a background of gray clouds, swollen and gross with unspilt rain. The snowy white horizontals of the padded guard ropes cut across him at knee and hip and shoulder line; otherwise his figure stands out clear, a relaxed, knobby figure, with tons of unexpended energy still held in reserve within it. The referee is close at hand, tolling off the inexorable tally of the count—"seven, eight, nine"—but scarcely is one cognizant of the referee's presence, of his arithmetic either. I see only that gnarled form lolling against the ropes, and eight feet away, the slighter, crumpled shape of the beaten Frenchman, with its kicking legs and its sobbing mouth, from which a little stream of blood runs down upon the lolled chin.

In a hush which instantaneously descends and as instantaneously is ended, the referee swings his arm down like a semaphore and chants out "ten."

The rest is a muddle and mass of confusion—Dempsey stooping over Carpentier as though wishful to lift him to his feet; then Dempsey encircled by a dozen policemen who for some reason feel called upon to surround him, two weeping French helpers dragging Carpentier to his corner and propping him upon a stool. Carpentier's long, slim legs dangling as they lift him and his feet slithering in futile fashion upon the resined canvas; Dempsey swinging his arms aloft in tardy token of appreciation for the whoops and cheers which flow toward him; all sorts of folks crowding into the ring; Dempsey marching out, convoyed by an entourage of his admirers; Carpentier, deadly pale, and most bewildered-looking with a forlorn, mechanical smile plastered on his face, shaking hands with somebody or other, and then the ring is empty of all save Humphries the orator, who announces a concluding bout between Billy Miske and Jack Renault.

As I settle back now to watch with languid interest this anticlimax, three things stand out in my memory as the high points of the big fight, so far as I personally am concerned.

The first is that Carpentier never had a chance. In the one round which properly belonged to him he fought himself out. He trusted to his strength when his refuge should have been in his speed.

The second is that vision of him, doubled up on his side, like a frightened, hurt boy, and yet striving to heave himself up and take added punishment from a foe against whom he had no shadow of hope.

The third—and most outstanding—will be my recollection of that look on Dempsey's towering front when realization came to him that a majority of the tremendous audience were partisans of the foreigner.

# Hub Fans Bid Kid Adieu

## John Updike

Here is a great piece of sports reporting that didn't come from
the press box. When Ted Williams played his last game for the
Red Sox at Fenway Park in Boston on September 28, 1960, one
of the spectators in the crowd along the third-base line was John
Updike, then twenty-eight years old, not long out of Harvard.
After writing this perceptive account of the Williams farewell
appearance, which was published in *The New Yorker*, Updike
went on to become a prominent novelist and literary critic and
never wrote about baseball again, even though he seems to have
a much deeper understanding of the game than most members
of the Baseball Writers Association of America.

Fenway Park, in Boston, is a lyric little bandbox of a ballpark.
Everything is painted green and seems in curiously sharp focus,
like the inside of an old-fashioned peeping-type Easter egg. It was
built in 1912 and rebuilt in 1934, and offers, as do most Boston
artifacts, a compromise between Man's Euclidean determinations
and Nature's beguiling irregularities. Its right field is one of the
deepest in the American League, while its left field is the shortest;
the high left-field wall, 315 feet from home plate along the foul
line, virtually thrusts its surface at right-handed hitters. On the
afternoon of Wednesday, September 28, 1960, as I took a seat
behind third base, a uniformed groundkeeper was treading the
top of this wall, picking batting-practice home runs out of the
screen, like a mushroom gatherer seen in Wordsworthian per-

spective on the verge of a cliff. The day was overcast, chill, and uninspirational. The Boston team was the worst in twenty-seven seasons. A jangling medley of incompetent youth and aging competence, the Red Sox were finishing in seventh place only because the Kansas City Athletics had locked them out of the cellar. They were scheduled to play the Baltimore Orioles, a much nimbler blend of May and December, who had been dumped from pennant contention a week before by the insatiable Yankees. I, and 10,453 others, had shown up primarily because this was the Red Sox's last home game of the season, and therefore the last time in all eternity that their regular left fielder, known to the headlines as TED, KID, SPLINTER, THUMPER, TW, and, most cloyingly, MISTER WONDERFUL, would play in Boston. "WHAT WILL WE DO WITHOUT TED? HUB FANS ASK" ran the headline on a newspaper being read by a bulb-nosed cigar smoker a few rows away. Williams' retirement had been announced, doubted (he had been threatening retirement for years), confirmed by Tom Yawkey, the Red Sox owner, and at last widely accepted as the sad but probable truth. He was forty-two and had redeemed his abysmal season of 1959 with a—considering his advanced age—fine one. He had been giving away his gloves and bats and had grudgingly consented to a sentimental ceremony today. This was not necessarily his last game; the Red Sox were scheduled to travel to New York and wind up the season with three games there.

The affair between Boston and Ted Williams has been no mere summer romance; it has been a marriage, composed of spats, mutual disappointments, and, toward the end, a mellowing hoard of shared memories. It falls into three stages, which may be termed Youth, Maturity, and Age; or Thesis, Antithesis, and Synthesis; or Jason, Achilles, and Nestor.

First, there was the by now legendary epoch when the young bridegroom came out of the West, announced "All I want out of life is that when I walk down the street folks will say, 'There goes the greatest hitter who ever lived.' " The dowagers of local journalism attempted to give elementary deportment lessons to this child who spake as a god, and to their horror were themselves rebuked. Thus began the long exchange of backbiting, bat-flipping, booing, and spitting that has distinguished Williams' public relations. The spitting incidents of 1957 and 1958 and the similar dockside courtesies that Williams has now and then extended to the grandstand should be judged against this background: the left-field stands at Fenway for twenty years have held a large number of customers who have bought their way in primarily for the privilege of showering abuse on Williams. Greatness necessarily attracts debunkers, but in Williams' case the hostility has been systematic and unappeasable. His basic offense against the fans has been to wish that they weren't there. Seeking a perfectionist's vacuum, he has quixotically desired to sever the game from the ground of paid spectatorship and publicity that supports it. Hence his refusal to tip his cap to the crowd or turn the other cheek to newsmen. It has been a costly theory—it has probably cost him, among other evidences of good will, two Most Valuable Player awards, which are voted by reporters—but he has held to it from his rookie year on. While his critics, oral and literary, remained beyond the reach of his discipline, the opposing pitchers were accessible, and he spanked them to the tune of .406 in 1941. He slumped to .356 in 1942 and went off to war.

In 1946, Williams returned from three years as a Marine pilot to the second of his baseball avatars, that of Achilles, the hero of incomparable prowess and beauty who nevertheless was to be found sulking in his tent while the Trojans (mostly Yankees) fought through to the ships. Yawkey, a timber and mining maharajah, had surrounded his central jewel with many gems of slightly lesser water, such as Bobby Doerr, Dom DiMaggio, Rudy York, Birdie Tebbetts, and Johnny Pesky. Throughout the late forties, the Red Sox were the best team in baseball on paper, yet they had little success on the field, and if this was a tragedy, Williams was Hamlet. A succinct review of the indictment—and a fair sample of appreciative sports-page prose—appeared the very day of Williams' valedictory, in a column by Huck Finnegan in the Boston *American* (no sentimentalist, Huck):

"Williams' career, in contrast [to Babe Ruth's], has been a series of failures except for his averages. He flopped in the only World Series he ever played in (1946) when he batted only .200. He flopped in the playoff game with Cleveland in 1948. He flopped in the final game of the 1949 season with the pennant hinging on the outcome (Yanks 5, Sox 3). He flopped in 1950 when he returned to the lineup after a two-month absence and ruined the morale of a club that seemed pennant-bound under Steve O'Neill. It has always been Williams' records first, the team second, and the Sox non-winning record is proof enough of that."

There are answers to all this, of course. The fatal weakness of the great Sox slugging teams was not-quite-good-enough pitching rather than Williams' failure to hit a home run every time he came to bat. Again, Williams' depressing effect on his teammates has never been proved. Despite ample coaching to the contrary, most insisted that they liked him. He has been generous with advice to any player who asked for it. In an increasingly combative baseball atmosphere, he continued to duck bean balls docilely. With umpires he was gracious to a fault. This courtesy itself annoyed his critics, whom there was no pleasing. And against the ten crucial games (the seven World Series games with the St. Louis Cardinals, the 1948 playoff with the Cleveland Indians, and the two-game series with the Yankees at the end of the 1949 season, winning either one of which would have given the Red Sox the pennant) that make up the Achilles' heel of Williams' record, a mass of statistics can be set showing that day in and day out he was no slouch in the clutch. The correspondence columns of the Boston papers now and then suffer a sharp flurry of arithmetic on this score; indeed, for Williams to have distributed all his hits so they did nobody else any good would constitute a feat of placement unparalleled in the annals of selfishness.

Whatever residue of truth remains of the Finnegan charge, those of us who love Williams must transmute as best we can, in our own personal crucibles. My personal memories of Williams begin when I was a boy in Pennsylvania, with two last-place teams

in Philadelphia to keep me company. For me, "W'ms, lf" was a
figment of the box scores who always seemed to be going 3-for-5.
He radiated, from afar, the hard blue glow of high purpose. I
remember listening over the radio to the All-Star Game of 1946, in
which Williams hit two singles and two home runs, the second one
off a Rip Sewell "blooper" pitch; it was like hitting a balloon out of
the park. I remember watching one of his home runs from the
bleachers of Shibe Park; it went over the first baseman's head and
rose meticulously along a straight line and was still rising when it
cleared the fence. The trajectory seemed qualitatively different
from anything anyone else might hit. For me, Williams is the
classic ballplayer of the game on a hot August weekday, before a
small crowd, when the only thing at stake is the tissue-thin difference between a thing done well and a thing done ill. Baseball is a
game of the long season, of relentless and gradual averaging-out.
Irrelevance—since the reference point of most individual games is
remote and statistical—always threatens its interest, which can be
maintained not by the occasional heroics that sportswriters feed
upon but by players who always care; who care, that is to say,
about themselves and their art. Insofar as the clutch hitter is not a
sportswriter's myth, he is a vulgarity, like a writer who writes only
for money. It may be that, compared to managers' dreams, such as
Joe DiMaggio and the always helpful Stan Musial, Williams is an
icy star. But of all team sports, baseball, with its graceful intermit-
tences of action, its immense and tranquil field sparsely settled
with poised men in white, its dispassionate mathematics, seems to
me best suited to accommodate, and be ornamented by, a loner. It
is essentially a lonely game. No other player visible to my generation has concentrated within himself so much of the sport's
poignance, has so assiduously refined his natural skills, has so
constantly brought to the plate that intensity of competence
that crowds the throat with joy.

By the time I went to college, near Boston, the lesser stars
Yawkey had assembled around Williams had faded, and his crafts-
manship, his rigorous pride, had become itself a kind of heroism.

This brittle and temperamental player developed an unexpected quality of persistence. He was always coming back—back from Korea, back from a broken collarbone, a shattered elbow, a bruised heel, back from drastic bouts of flu and ptomaine poisoning. Hardly a season went by without some enfeebling mishap, yet he always came back, and always looked like himself. The delicate mechanism of timing and power seemed locked, shockproof, in some case outside his body. In addition to injuries, there were a heavily publicized divorce, and the usual storms with the press, and the Williams Shift—the maneuver, custom-built by Lou Boudreau, of the Cleveland Indians, whereby three infielders were concentrated on the right side of the infield, where a left-handed pull hitter like Williams generally hits the ball. Williams could easily have learned to punch singles through the vacancy on his left and fattened his average hugely. This was what Ty Cobb told him to do. But the game had changed since Cobb; Williams believed that his value to the club and to the game was as a slugger, so he went on pulling the ball, trying to blast it through three men, and paid the price of perhaps fifteen points of lifetime average. Like Ruth before him, he bought the occasional home run at the cost of many directed singles—a calculated sacrifice certainly not, in the case of a hitter as average-minded as Williams, entirely selfish.

After a prime so harassed and hobbled, Williams was granted by the relenting fates a golden twilight. He became at the end of his career perhaps the best old hitter of the century. The dividing line came between the 1956 and 1957 seasons. In September of the first year, he and Mickey Mantle were contending for the batting championship. Both were hitting around .350, and there was no one else near them. The season ended with a three-game series between the Yankees and the Sox, and, living in New York then, I went up to the Stadium. Williams was slightly shy of the four hundred at-bats needed to qualify; the fear was expressed that the Yankee pitchers would walk him to protect Mantle. Instead, they pitched to him—a wise decision. He looked terrible at the plate, tired and discouraged and unconvincing. He never looked very good to me in the Stadium. (Last week, in *Life*, Williams, a sportswriter himself now, wrote gloomily of the Stadium, "There's the bigness of it. There are those high stands and all those people smoking—and, of course, the shadows . . . It takes at least one Series to get accustomed to the Stadium and even then you're not sure.") The final outcome in 1956 was Mantle .353, Williams .345.

The next year, I moved from New York to New England, and it made all the difference. For in September of 1957, in the same situation, the story was reversed. Mantle finally hit .365; it was the best season of his career. But Williams, though sick and old, had run away from him. A bout of flu had laid him low in September. He emerged from his cave in the Hotel Somerset haggard but irresistible; he hit four successive pinch-hit home runs. "I feel terrible," he confessed, "but every time I take a swing at the ball it goes out of the park." He ended the season with thirty-eight home runs and an average of .388, the highest in either league since his own .406, and, coming from a decrepit man of thirty-nine, an even more supernal figure. With eight or so of the "leg hits" that a younger man would have beaten out, it would have been .400. And the next year, Williams, who in 1949 and 1953 had lost batting championships by decimal whiskers to George Kell and Mickey Vernon, sneaked in behind his teammate Pete Runnels and filched his sixth title, a bargain at .328.

In 1959, it seemed all over. The dinosaur thrashed around in the .200 swamp for the first half of the season, and was even benched ("rested," Manager Mike Higgins tactfully said). Old foes like the late Bill Cunningham thought Williams was jiggling his elbows; in truth, Williams' neck was so stiff he could hardly turn his head to look at the pitcher. When he swung, it looked like a Calder mobile with one thread cut; it reminded you that since 1953 Williams' shoulders had been wired together. A solicitous pall settled over the sports pages. In the two decades since Williams had come to Boston, his status had imperceptibly shifted from that of a naughty prodigy to that of a municipal monument. As his shadow in the

record books lengthened, the Red Sox teams around him de-
clined, and the entire American League seemed to be losing life
and color to the National. The inconsistency of the new super-
stars—Mantle, Colavito, and Kaline—served to make Williams
appear all the more singular. And off the field, his private
philanthropy—in particular, his zealous chairmanship of the
Jimmy Fund, a charity for children with cancer—gave him a civic
presence somewhat like that of Richard Cardinal Cushing. In
religion, Williams appears to be a humanist, and a selective one at
that, but he and the Cardinal, when their good works intersect and
they appear in the public eye together, make a handsome and
heartening pair.

Humiliated by his '59 season, Williams determined, once more,
to come back. I, as a specimen Williams partisan, was both glad
and fearful. All baseball fans believed in miracles; the question is,
how many do you believe in? He looked like a ghost in spring
training. Manager Jurges warned us ahead of time that if Williams
didn't come through he would be benched, just like anybody else.
As it turned out, it was Jurges who was benched. Williams entered
the 1960 season needing eight home runs to have a lifetime total of
500; after one time at bat in Washington, he needed seven. For a
stretch, he was hitting a home run every second game that he
played. The summer was a statistician's picnic. His two-thou-
sandth walk came and went, his eighteen-hundredth run batted
in, his sixteenth All-Star Game. At one point, he hit a home run off
a pitcher, Don Lee, off whose father, Thornton Lee, he had hit a
home run a generation before. The only comparable season for a
forty-two-year-old man was Ty Cobb's in 1928. Cobb batted .323
and hit one homer. Williams batted .316 but hit twenty-nine
homers. . . .

The batting cage was trundled away. The Orioles fluttered to
the sidelines. Diagonally across the field, by the Red Sox dugout, a
cluster of men in overcoats were festering like maggots. I could see
a splinter of white uniform, and Williams' head, held at a self-dep-
recating and evasive tilt. Williams' conversational stance is that

of a six-foot-three-inch man under a six-foot ceiling. He moved away to the patter of flash bulbs, and began playing catch with a young Negro outfielder named Willie Tasby. His arm, never very powerful, had grown lax with the years, and his throwing motion was a kind of muscular drawl. To catch the ball, he flicked his glove hand onto his left shoulder (he batted left but threw right, as every schoolboy ought to know) and let the ball plop into it comically. This catch session with Tasby was the only time all afternoon I saw him grin.

A tight little flock of human sparrows who, from the lambent and pampered pink of their faces, could only have been Boston politicians moved toward the plate. The loudspeakers mammothly coughed as someone huffed on the microphone. The ceremonies began. Curt Gowdy, the Red Sox radio and television announcer, who sounds like everybody's brother-in-law, delivered a brief sermon, taking the two words "pride" and "champion" as his text. It began, "Twenty-one years ago, a skinny kid from San Diego, California . . ." and ended, "I don't think we'll ever see another like him." Robert Tibolt, chairman of the board of the Greater Boston Chamber of Commerce, presented Williams with a big Paul Revere silver bowl, Harry Carlson, a member of the sports committee of the Boston Chamber, gave him a plaque, whose inscription he did not read in its entirety, out of deference to Williams' distaste for this sort of fuss. Mayor Collins presented the Jimmy Fund with a thousand-dollar check.

Then the occasion himself stooped to the microphone, and his voice sounded, after the others, very Californian; it seemed to be coming, excellently amplified, from a great distance, adolescently young and as smooth as a butternut. His thanks for the gifts had not died from our ears before he glided, as if helplessly, into "In spite of all the terrible things that have been said about me by the maestros of the keyboard up there . . ." He glanced up at the press rows suspended above home plate. (All the Boston reporters, incidentally, reported the phrase as "knights of the keyboard," but I heard it as "maestros" and prefer it that way.) The crowd tittered, appalled. A frightful vision flashed upon me, of the press gallery pelting Williams with erasers, of Williams clambering up the foul screen to slug journalists, of a riot, of Mayor Collins being crushed. ". . . And they were terrible things," Williams insisted, with level melancholy, into the mike. "I'd like to forget them, but I can't." He paused, swallowed his memories, and went on, "I want to say that my years in Boston have been the greatest thing in my life." The crowd, like an immense sail going limp in a change of wind, sighed with relief. Taking all the parts himself, Williams then acted out a vivacious little morality drama in which an imaginary tempter came to him at the beginning of his career and said, "Ted, you can play anywhere you like." Leaping nimbly into the role of his younger self (who in biographical actuality had yearned to be a Yankee), Williams gallantly chose Boston over all the other cities, and told us that Tom Yawkey was the greatest owner in baseball and we were the greatest fans. We applauded ourselves heartily. The umpire came out and dusted the plate. The voice of doom announced over the loudspeakers that after Williams' retirement his uniform number, 9, would be permanently retired—the first time the Red Sox had so honored a player. We cheered. The national anthem was played. We cheered. The game began.

Williams was third in the batting order, so he came up in the bottom of the first inning, and Steve Barber, a young pitcher who was not yet born when Williams began playing for the Red Sox, offered him four pitches, at all of which he disdained to swing, since none of them were within the strike zone. This demonstrated simultaneously that Williams' eyes were razor-sharp and that Barber's control wasn't. Shortly, the bases were full, with Williams on second. "Oh, I hope he gets held up at third! That would be wonderful," the girl beside me moaned, and, sure enough, the man at bat walked and Williams was delivered into our foreground. He struck the pose of Donatello's David, the third-base bag being Goliath's head. Fiddling with his cap, swapping small talk with the Oriole third baseman (who seemed delighted to have him drop in), swinging his arms with a sort of prancing nervousness, he looked fine—flexible, hard, and not unbecomingly substantial through the middle. The long neck, the small head, the knickers whose cuffs were worn down near his ankles—all these points, often observed by caricaturists, were visible in the flesh.

One of the collegiate voices behind me said, "He looks old, doesn't he, old; big deep wrinkles in his face . . ."

"Yeah," the other voice said, "but he looks like an old hawk, doesn't he?"

With each pitch, Williams danced down the baseline, waving his arms and stirring dust, ponderous but menacing, like an attacking goose. It occurred to about a dozen humorists at once to shout, "Steal home! Go, go!" Williams' speed afoot was never legendary. Lou Clinton, a young Sox outfielder, hit a fairly deep fly to center field. Williams tagged up and ran home. As he slid across the plate, the ball, thrown with unusual heft by Jackie Brandt, the Oriole center fielder, hit him on the back.

"Boy, he was really loafing, wasn't he?" one of the boys behind me said.

"It's cold," the other explained. "He doesn't play well when it's cold. He likes heat. He's a hedonist."

Whenever Williams appeared at the plate—pounding the dirt from his cleats, gouging a pit in the batter's box with his left foot, wringing resin out of the bat handle with his vehement grip, switching the stick at the pitcher with an electric ferocity—it was like having a familiar Leonardo appear in a shuffle of *Saturday Evening Post* covers. This man, you realized—and here, perhaps, was the difference, greater than the difference in gifts—really intended to hit the ball. In the third inning, he hoisted a high fly to deep center. In the fifth, we thought he had it; he smacked the ball hard and high into the heart of his power zone, but the deep right field in Fenway and the heavy air and a casual east wind defeated him. The ball died. Al Pilarcik leaned his back against the big "380" painted on the right-field wall and caught it. On another day, in another park, it would have been gone. (After the game, Williams said, "I didn't think I could hit one any harder than that. The conditions weren't good.")

The afternoon grew so glowering that in the sixth inning the arc lights were turned on—always a wan sight in the daytime, like the burning headlights of a funeral procession. Williams did not come to bat in the seventh. He was second up in the eighth. This was almost certainly his last time to come to the plate in Fenway Park, and instead of merely cheering, as we had at his three previous appearances, we stood, all of us—stood and applauded. Have you ever heard applause in a ball park? Just applause—no calling, no whistling, just an ocean of handclaps, minute after minute, burst after burst, crowding and running together in continuous succession like the pushes of surf at the edge of the sand. It was a somber and considered tumult. There was not a boo in it. It seemed to renew itself out of a shifting set of memories as the kid, the Marine, the veteran of feuds and failures and injuries, the friend of children, and the enduring old pro evolved down the bright tunnel of twenty-one summers toward this moment. Only Williams had moved during the ovation, switching his bat impatiently, ignoring everything except his cherished task. The pitcher wound up, and the applause sank into a hush.

Understand that we were a crowd of rational people. We knew that a home run cannot be produced at will; the right pitch must be perfectly met and luck must ride with the ball. Three innings before, we had seen a brave effort fail. The air was soggy; the season was exhausted. Nevertheless, there will always lurk, around a corner in a pocket of our knowledge of the odds, an indefensible hope, and this was one of the times, which you now and then find in sports, when a density of expectation hangs in the air.

Jack Fisher, who was now pitching, was wide with the first pitch. He put the second one over, and Williams swung mightily and missed. The crowd grunted, seeing that classic swing, so long and smooth and quick, exposed, naked in its failure. Fisher threw the third time. Williams swung again and there it was. The ball climbed on a diagonal line into the vast volume of air over center field. From my angle, behind third base, the ball seemed less an object in flight than the tip of a towering, motionless construct, like the Eiffel Tower or the Tappan Zee Bridge. It was in the books while it was still in the sky. Brandt ran back to the deepest corner of the outfield grass; the ball descended beyond his reach and struck in the crotch where the bullpen met the wall, bounced chunkily, and, as far as I could see, vanished.

Like a feather caught in a vortex, Williams ran around the square of bases at the center of our beseeching screaming. He ran as he always ran out home runs—hurriedly, unsmiling, head down, as if our praise were a storm of rain to get out of. He didn't tip his cap. Though we thumped, wept, and chanted, "We want Ted," for minutes after he hid in the dugout, he did not come back. Our noise for some seconds passed beyond excitement into a kind of immense open anguish, a wailing, a cry to be saved. But immortality is nontransferable. The papers said that the other players, and even the umpires on the field, begged him to come out and acknowledge us in some way, but he never had and did not now. Gods do not answer letters.

Every true story has an anticlimax. The men on the field refused to disappear, as would have seemed decent, in the smoke of Williams' miracle. Fisher continued to pitch, and escaped further harm. At the end of the inning, Higgins sent Williams out to his left-field position, then instantly replaced him with Carrol Hardy, so we had a long last look at Williams as he ran out there and then back, his uniform jogging, his eyes steadfast on the ground. It was nice, and we were grateful, but it left a funny taste.

One of the scholasticists behind me said, "Let's go. We've seen everything. I don't want to spoil it." This seemed a sound aesthetic decision. Williams' last word had been so exquisitely chosen, such a perfect fusion of expectation, intention, and execution, that already it felt a little unreal in my head, and I wanted to get out before the castle collapsed. But the game, though played by clumsy midgets under the feeble glow of the arc lights, began to tug at my attention, and I loitered in the runway until it was over. Williams' homer had, quite incidentally, made the score 4–3. In the bottom of the ninth inning, with one out, Marlin Coughtry, the second-base juggler, singled. Vic Wertz, pinch-hitting, doubled off the left-field wall, Coughtry advancing to third. Pumpsie Green walked to load the bases. Willie Tasby hit a double-play ball to the third baseman, but in making the pivot throw Billy Klaus, an ex–Red Sox infielder, reverted to form and threw the ball past the first baseman and into the Red Sox dugout. The Sox won, 5–4. On the car radio as I drove home, I heard that Williams had decided not to accompany the team to New York. So he knew how to do even that, the hardest thing. Quit.

# The Long Count
## *Gene Tunney*

Gene Tunney, the undefeated heavyweight champion, is one of
the few professional boxers with a lively interest in writing and
literature. He was friendly with George Bernard Shaw and once
lectured on Shakespeare at Yale. This account of his two fights
with Jack Dempsey and his recovery from the one and only
knockdown of his ring career—and how he spent seven years
planning and preparing himself physically for those fights
—must be one of the most interesting stories in the literature of
boxing. There are those who may doubt Tunney's simple explanation of why he failed to see Dempsey's big left-hand punch
coming, but that doesn't make his recollections any less engrossing.

The laugh of the Twenties was my confident insistence that I
would defeat Jack Dempsey for the heavyweight championship of
the world. To the boxing public, this optimistic belief was the
funniest of jokes. To me, it was a reasonable statement of calculated probability, an opinion based on prize-ring logic.

The logic went back to a day in 1919, to a boat trip down the
Rhine River. After the First World War, the Army sent a group of
A.E.F. athletes to the German Rhineland to give exhibitions for
doughboys in the American occupation forces. I was the light-
heavyweight boxing champion of the A.E.F. Sailing past castles on
the Rhine, I was talking with the corporal in charge of the party.
Corporal McReynolds was a peacetime sportswriter in Joplin,
Missouri, one of those Midwestern newspapermen who combined
talent with a copious assortment of knowledge. He had a consum-
mate understanding of boxing, and I was asking him a question of
wide interest in the A.E.F. of those days.

We had been hearing about a new prizefighting phenomenon in the United States, a battler burning up the ring back home. He was to meet Jess Willard for the heavyweight championship. His name was Jack Dempsey. None of us knew anything about him, his rise to the challenging position for the title had been so swift. What about him? What was he like? American soldiers were all interested in prizefighting, I more so than most—an A.E.F. boxer with some idea of continuing my ring career in civilian life.

The Corporal said yes, he knew Jack Dempsey. He had seen Dempsey box a number of times, and had covered the bouts for his Midwestern paper.

"Is he good?" I inquired.

"He's tops," responded Corporal McReynolds. "He'll murder Willard."

"What's he like?" I asked.

The Corporal's reply was vividly descriptive. It won't mean anything to most people nowadays, but at that time it was completely descriptive to anyone who read the sports pages. McReynolds said: "He's a big Jack Dillon."

I knew about Jack Dillon, as who didn't in those days? He was a middleweight with a destructive assault—fast, shifty, hard-hitting, weaving in with short savage punches, a knocker-out, a killer. Dillon looked like Dempsey, swarthy, beetle-browed, and grim.

I thought it over for a moment and said, "Jack Dillon was beaten by Mike Gibbons, wasn't he?"

"Yes," the Corporal replied. "I saw that bout. Gibbons was too good a boxer. He was too fast. His defense was too good. Dillon couldn't lay a glove on him."

Mike Gibbons was the master boxer of his time, the height of defensive skill, a perfectionist in the art of sparring.

I said to the Corporal, "Well, maybe Jack Dempsey can be beaten by clever boxing."

His reply was reflective, thought out. "Yes," he said. "When Dempsey is beaten, a fast boxer with a good defense will do it."

This, coming from a sportswriter who had studied the style of Dempsey, started me thinking. My ambition was to become skilled in boxing, speed and defense, on the order of Mike Gibbons.

As a kid on the West Side of New York City fooling around with boxing gloves, I had been, for some reason of temperament, more interested in dodging a blow than in striking one. Fighting in preliminary bouts around New York, I had learned the value of skill in sparring. In A.E.F. boxing I had emphasized skill and defense because during that time I had hurt my hands. With damaged fists I had reason to cultivate defensive sparring.

Sailing down the Rhine that day, I thought that maybe some time in the future I might be a big Mike Gibbons facing a big Jack Dillon. It was my first thought that some day I might defeat Jack Dempsey for the heavyweight championship of the world, which all fans then assumed Jack was about to acquire.

This thought stuck in my mind. Presently the time came when I was able to observe Dempsey firsthand. I was one of the preliminary boxers on the card of the Dempsey-Carpentier fight in 1921. I fought in the semi-final bout. This place of honor and profit was given to me because of my armed service title. The light heavyweight championship of the A.E.F. brought me publicity in that postwar period. I was ballyhooed as "The Fighting Marine."

Actually I had no business being in the second billed bout on that card of the first Million Dollar Gate. I may have been an A.E.F. champ, but we boxers in the service knew well enough that our style of pugilism was feeble and amateurish compared to that of the professionals. The best of us were mere preliminary fighters, as I was then. There were mighty few accomplished boxers in Pershing's A.E.F. Later, in World War II, there were champs and near-champs in uniform, but the draft was not so all-embracing during the war against the Kaiser.

In that semi-final bout on the day of the Dempsey-Carpentier extravaganza, I fought poorly. My injured hands were still bothering me. Nobody there that day could have pictured me as a future conqueror of the devastating champ, least of all Jack himself, if he had taken any notice of the semi-final battlers. I won on a technical K.O. from my opponent, Soldier Jones of Canada, only because he was so bad. Like myself, he was in the big show on an army title, his wartime service record covering a multitude of sins.

After the bout, clad in my bathrobe, I crouched at one corner of the ring and watched Dempsey exchange blows with Carpentier. The champion was in every respect a big Jack Dillon. No wonder, I thought, that they call him the Man Killer. But studying his moves intently, I saw enough to confirm Corporal McReynolds' estimate that when Dempsey was defeated it would be by a skillful defensive boxer, a big Mike Gibbons. Correct defense, I thought, could foil the shattering Dempsey attack.

Dempsey's next fight at Shelby, Montana, was against Tom Gibbons, the heavyweight younger brother of Mike. Tom, like Mike, was a skilled boxer. Dempsey couldn't knock him out. The public, which had considered Tom Gibbons an easy mark, was incredulous and assumed that there was something peculiar about the fight. To me, it was not peculiar, just proof that a good boxer could thwart Dempsey.

At the Dempsey-Carpentier fight I had noticed something that stayed in my mind for years afterwards. In the second round, Carpentier had thrown a right hand punch, hitting Dempsey high on the jaw with all of his power. I was in a position at the ringside to see the punch clearly and to note how Carpentier had thrown it. He drew back his right hand like a pitcher about to throw a baseball. The news that the punch was coming was telegraphed all over the stadium. Yet it landed on a vulnerable spot. How anybody could be hit with a right launched like that one was mystifying to anybody who understood boxing. Dempsey went back on his heels, jarred. Carpentier couldn't follow up on this advantage, and a moment later, Jack had recovered and was back again on the job of wrecking Carpentier with body blows. But the landing of that one blow demonstrated vividly to me that Dempsey could be hit with a hard right.

Dempsey was no protective boxer, not a defensive sparrer. His kind of defense was shifty moving. He couldn't be hit with just any punch, but I saw that he could be nailed with a straight right. This weakness was confirmed in his later bout with the clumsy but powerful Luis Firpo, who knocked Dempsey out of the ring with right-hand punches and almost won the championship. That to me signified that Dempsey could be beaten by a combination of defensive boxing and a right-hand punch that had everything thrown into it. It would never do for me, or anybody else, to mix it up with Dempsey in an exchange of haymakers. The right-hand blow that I was thinking about would have to come to him as a surprise. And coming from a boxer of my style, if we ever did meet, such a right-hander would be a surprise. Jack would never expect a Sunday punch from me. I was catalogued not only as a defensive boxer but as a light hitter, with no hard punch. I was known as a fighter who might wear an opponent down and cut him to pieces but it was assumed that I couldn't knock anybody out. That was true—at that time—because I had been handicapped by bad hands. I could hit hard enough in 1921 but I did not dare to do so for fear of breaking my hands. So I was a comparatively light hitter, and I was typed as such in the boxing business.

To strengthen my hands, I went to a lumber camp in Canada and worked for one winter as a woodsman, chopping down trees. The months of wood chopping and other hand exercises made my hands strong and hard, my fists rugged enough to take the impact of the most powerful blow that I could land. From then on I had little trouble, and no fears about my hands, but I was still tagged in the boxing circles as a feather duster puncher. I used that reputation to my advantage in later bouts. At the beginning of the first round, I would put everything I had behind a right-hand punch. If I didn't score a knockout, the blow would daze the other man sufficiently to make it easy for me to outbox him the rest of the way.

Soon I was fighting my way to a challenger's position. I won the light heavyweight championship from Harry Greb, one of the

greatest pugilists, and went on to establish myself as a heavyweight contender by defeating Tom Gibbons. Public opinion on
my chances against Dempsey was loud and summary. He was
considered unbeatable and I was rated as a victim doomed to
obliteration, pathetic and absurd.

It was argued that I was a synthetic fighter. That was true. As a
kid preliminary battler, I had held a shipping clerk's job with a
steamship company to earn a living. I boxed only for the love of the
game. As a marine in France, I boxed to avoid irksome military
duties after the armistice. After the war, when I developed sparring ability as a means of making money, it was said that I lacked
the killer instinct. That was also true. I found no joy in knocking
anybody unconscious. I had a notion that the so-called killer
instinct was really based on fear, that the killer in the ring raged
with brutality because down deep he was afraid. So I was a
synthetic fighter, built by training and conditioning, without a
true fighter's killer instinct. People might have noted that while
Dempsey had failed to flatten Tom Gibbons, I had knocked him
out. But then the Dempsey-Gibbons bout was dismissed as mystifying, one of "those things."

The prize fight experts were almost unanimous in not giving me
a chance against Dempsey. There were, so far as I know, only a few
persons prominent in sports who thought I might win and said so.

When Dempsey and I got into the ring for our first fight in
Philadelphia in 1926, things went so closely according to my plan
that the bout was almost unexciting for me. During the first few
minutes of sparring, I feinted Dempsey a couple of times and then
lashed out with a right-hand punch, the hardest blow I ever threw.
It failed to knock him out. Jack was a hard man to flatten. His
fighting style made it difficult to tag him on the jaw. He fought in a
crouch with his chin tucked down behind his left shoulder. I hit
him high, on the cheek. He was shaken and dazed. His strength,
speed and accuracy were reduced. Thereafter it was just a matter
of outboxing him, foiling his rushes, piling up points, clipping him
with repeated, damaging blows, and sparring correctly.

There was one unexpected element—rain. It drizzled and showered intermittently throughout the fight. The ring was wet and slippery, the footing insecure. That was bad for a boxer like me. On the other hand, the slippery ring also worked to Dempsey's disadvantage. Jack was battered and worn at the end of the scheduled ten rounds. I might have knocked him out if the bout had gone a few rounds more. The decision was unanimous, and I was the heavyweight champion of the world.

The real argument of the decade grew out of my second bout with Dempsey, at Chicago—the "long count" controversy. It produced endless talk, sense and nonsense, logic and illogic. To this day in any barroom you can work up a wrangle on the subject of the long count. How long was Tunney on the floor after Dempsey knocked him down? Could he have gotten up if the count had been normal?

To me the mystery has always been how Dempsey contrived to hit me as he did. In a swirl of action, a wild mix-up with things happening fast, Jack might have nailed the most perfect boxer that ever blocked or sidestepped a punch, he was that swift and accurate a hitter. But what happened to me did not occur in any dizzy confusion of flying fists. In an ordinary exchange Dempsey simply stepped in and hit me with a left hook.

It was in the seventh round. I had been outboxing Jack all the way. He hadn't hurt me, hadn't hit me with any effect. I wasn't dazed or tired. I was sparring in my best form, when he lashed out.

For a boxer of any skill to be hit with a left swing in a commonplace maneuver of sparring is sheer disgrace. It was Dempsey's most effective blow, the one thing you'd watch for—you'd better, for the Dempsey left, as prize-ring history relates, was murder. I knew how to evade it, sidestep or jab him with a left and beat him to the punch. I had been doing that all along.

I didn't see the left coming. So far as I was concerned, it came out of nowhere. That embarrassed me more than anything else —not to mention the damage done. It was a blow to pride as well as to the jaw. I was vain of my eyesight. My vision in the ring was

always excellent. I used to think I could see a punch coming almost
before it started. If there was anything I could rely on, it was my
sharpness of eye—and I utterly failed to see that left swing.

The only explanation I have ever been able to think of is that in a
training bout I had sustained an injury to my right eye. A sparring
partner had poked me in the eye with thumb extended. I was
rendered completely blind for an instant, and after some medi-
cal treatment was left with astigmatism which would easily
have caused a blind spot, creating an area in which there was no
vision. Our relative positions, when Dempsey hit me, must have
been such that the left swing came up into the blind spot, and I
never saw it.

With all his accuracy and power Dempsey hit me flush on the
jaw, the button. I was knocked dizzy. Whereupon he closed for
the kill, and that meant fighting fury at its most destructive. When
Dempsey came in for a knockout he came with all his speed and
power. I didn't know then how many times he slugged me. I had to
look at the motion pictures the next day to find out. There were
seven crashing blows, Dempsey battering me with left and right as
I fell against the ropes, collapsing to a sitting position on the
canvas.

Of what ensued during the next few seconds, I knew nothing. I
was oblivious of the most debated incident of the long count and
had to be told later on what happened.

The story went back to the Dempsey-Firpo fight, to that wild
first round during which Firpo hit the floor in one knock-down
after another. This was in New York, where the rule was that a
boxer scoring a knock-down must go to a neutral corner and
remain there until the referee had completed the count. In the
ring with the Wild Bull of the Pampas, Dempsey undoubtedly
through excitement of battle violated that rule, as the motion
pictures showed clearly afterward.

Jack confesses he remembers nothing that took place during
that entire fight. Firpo landed a terrific first blow. Dempsey, after
suffering a first-blow knock-down, apparently jumped up to the

fray by sheer professional instinct—the fighting heart of a true champion. Instead of going to a corner, Jack would stand over Firpo and slug him as he got up. After one knock-down, Jack stepped over his prostrate opponent to the other side, to get a better shot at him—the referee was in the way. After another knock-down, Dempsey slugged Firpo before the South American had got his hands off the floor, when he was still technically down. The Champ might well have been disqualified for that—not to mention the fact that he was pushed back into the ring when Firpo battered him out. The referee, however, in his confusion permitted all the violations.

The Dempsey-Firpo brawl aroused a storm of protest and brought about a determination that in the future Dempsey should be kept strictly to the rules. In our Chicago bout the regulation applied—go to a neutral corner upon scoring a knock-down. The referee had been especially instructed to enforce this. He was told that, in case of a knock-down, he was not to begin a count until the boxer who had scored the knock-down had gone to a neutral corner.

This was the reason for the long count. Dempsey, having battered me to the canvas, stood over me to hit me the moment I got up—if I did get up. The referee ordered him to a neutral corner. He didn't go. The referee, in accordance with instructions, refrained from giving count until he did go. That imposed on Jack a penalty of four seconds. It was that long before he went to the corner and the referee began the count.

When I regained full consciousness, the count was at two, I knew nothing of what had gone on, was only aware that the referee was counting two over me. What a surprise! I had eight seconds in which to get up. My head was clear. I had trained hard and well, as I always did, and had that invaluable asset—condition. In the proverbial pink, I recovered quickly from the shock of the battering I had taken. I thought—what now? I'd take the full count, of course. Nobody but a fool fails to do that. I felt all right, and had no doubt about being able to get up. The question was what to do when I was back on my feet.

I never had been knocked down before. In all the ring battles and training bouts I had engaged in, I had never previously been on the canvas. But I had always thought about the possibility, and had always planned before each bout what to do if I were knocked down, what strategy to use upon getting up. That depended on the kind of opponent.

I had thought the question out carefully in the case of Jack Dempsey. If he were to knock me down, he would, when I got up, rush me to apply the finisher. He would be swift and headlong about it. Should I try to clinch and thus gain some seconds of breathing space? That's familiar strategy for a boxer after a knockdown. Often it's the correct strategy—but not against Dempsey, I figured. He hit too hard and fast with short punches for it to be at all safe to close for a clinch. He might knock me out.

Another possibility was to get set and hit him as he rushed. That can be effective against a fighter who, having scored a knockdown, comes tearing in wide open, a mark for a heavy blow. If you are strong upon getting to your feet, you can sometimes turn the tables by throwing everything into a punch. Bob Fitzsimmons often did it. But that wouldn't do against Dempsey, I reckoned. He was too tough and hit too hard. He would welcome a slugging match. After having been knocked down, I might not be in any shape to take the risk of stepping in and hitting him.

For my second bout with Dempsey the plan that I decided upon, in case I was knocked down, was based on the thing I had learned about Jack. Word from his training camp had indicated that his legs were none too good. I had learned that his trainers had been giving him special exercises for footwork, because he had slowed down in the legs. That was the cue—match my legs against his, keep away from him, depend on speed of foot, let him chase me until I was sure I had recovered completely from the knockdown.

The plan would work if my own legs were in good shape, after the battering I had taken. That was what I had to think about on the floor in Chicago. My legs felt all right. At the count of nine I got up. My legs felt strong and springy.

Jack came tearing in for the kill. I stepped away from him,
moving to my left—circling away from his left hook. As I sidestepped swiftly, my legs had never been better. What I had heard
about Dempsey's legs was true. As I circled away from him, he
tried doggedly, desperately, to keep up with me—but he was
slow. The strategy was okay—keep away from him until I was
certain that all the effects of the knock-down had worn off. Once,
in sheer desperation, Jack stopped in his tracks and growled at me
to stand and fight.

I did—but later, when I knew that my strength, speed, and
reflexes were completely normal. I started to close with him and
hit him with the encyclopedia of boxing. Presently Dempsey's legs
were so heavy that he couldn't move with any agility at all, and I
was able to hit him virtually at will. He was almost helpless when
the final bell rang—sticking it out with stubborn courage.

I have often been asked—could I have gotten up and carried on
as I did without those extra four seconds of the long count? I don't
know. I can only say that at the count of two I came to, and felt in
good shape. I had eight seconds to go. Without the long count, I
would have had four seconds to go. Could I, in that space of time,
have gotten up? I'm quite sure that I could have. When I regained
consciousness after the brief period of blackout, I felt that I could
have jumped up immediately and matched my legs against Jack's,
just as I did.

The long count controversy, with all the heated debate, produced a huge public demand for another Dempsey-Tunney fight,
number three. Tex Rickard was eager to stage it. He knew, as
everybody else did, that it would draw the biggest gate ever. The
first Dempsey-Tunney fight grossed over a million seven hundred
thousand; the second, over two million and a half. Rickard was
sure a third would draw three million. I was willing, eager. I
planned to retire after another championship bout, wanted to get
all that I could out of it.

But Jack refused. He was afraid of going blind. The battering he
had taken around the eyes in his two fights with me alarmed him.

The very thing that kept him from being hit on the jaw, his style of holding his chin down behind his shoulder, caused punches to land high. He dreaded the horror that has befallen so many ring fighters and is the terror of them all—the damage that comes from too many punches around the eyes, blindness.

Jack Dempsey was a great fighter—possibly the greatest that ever entered a ring. Looking back objectively, one has to conclude that he was more valuable to the sport or "The Game" than any prizefighter of his time. Whether you consider it from his worth as a gladiator or from the point of view of the box office, he was tops. His name in his most glorious days was magic among his people, and today, twenty years after, the name Jack Dempsey is still magic. This tells a volume in itself. As one who has always had pride in his profession as well as his professional theories, and possessing a fair share of Celtic romanticism, I wish that we could have met when we were both at our unquestionable best. We could have decided many questions, to me the most important of which is whether "a good boxer can always lick a good fighter."

I still say yes.

# Knute Rockne, the Man and the Legend

## *Jack Newcombe*

The most inspiring football coach who ever gave a fight talk in a locker room, Knute Rockne of Notre Dame had reached a height in his profession before his death in a 1931 plane crash that has never been approached by anyone else. During his twelve seasons as head coach at South Bend, his teams won 105 games, tied five, and lost twelve. In five of those years, Notre Dame was unbeaten and untied. After Jack Newcombe wrote this profile of Rockne for *Sport* magazine in 1953, the editor, Al Silverman, said of it, "We knew it was good—but we didn't realize how good, until Notre Dame men began writing in saying that it was the best story ever written about the Rock."

During his fabulous football coaching career at Notre Dame, Knute Rockne was surrounded by a legend that has grown with the years until it has become hard to view the man as he really was. Like the stories of the lives of so many great men, Rockne's has been distorted in the retelling, stretched out of its honest shape by those who knew him only as an immortal figure of the so-called Golden Age of sports, and, too, by some of those who knew him and loved him best. You can't blame them. Rockne was a man of such bounding wit and dynamic personality that stories naturally sprouted around him wherever he went. Some of them were planted by Rockne himself in the banquet halls where he was always in demand as a speaker. Many of them were leaked out of the locker room and from the practice lots at Notre Dame where he sometimes exercised a godlike influence on the boys who played for him. In this age of skepticism it would be easy to discredit them, to write them all off as part of the Rockne myth. But it is just as wrong to debunk the whole Rockne story as it is to swallow it anecdote by anecdote.

Who was Knute Rockne?

He was the head coach of football at Notre Dame from 1918 through 1930. His teams won 105 games, lost 12 and tied five. Five of them completed unbeaten, untied seasons. As recently as 1951, the Associated Press, in a nationwide poll, named him coach of the all-time All-America football team. He was a pioneer in football, an advocate of mobile, swift-striking teams in a time when other coaches stressed raw beef and power. He was the most influential and articulate defender of the college sport when it fell under public criticism. He was such a witty speaker that Will Rogers once said, "I would have hated to follow him on any banquet program. He told me many stories, and I retold them and got a lot of laughs. If there was anyone I owed royalties to, it was Rock."

Rockne spoiled the locker-room pep talk for all the coaches who followed him. None could match him in the art of pumping spirit into the troops before the kick-off. He could get his players so screaming mad at themselves, or at him, that they all but tore the locker-room door off its hinges as they exploded onto the field. Or he could fill them with such sticky sentiment that there wouldn't be a dry eye in the room. Either technique made it hard on the other team.

One of Rockne's classic locker-room performances took place at halftime in the 1925 Northwestern–Notre Dame game at South Bend. The Irish had not lost a home game in 20 years but midway through this one it seemed certain that record would be broken. Northwestern was leading, 10 to 0. The story of what took place in the Notre Dame dressing room during the halftime intermission has been retold in many versions. Joe Boland later gave an eyewitness account. He was the first-string left tackle on that Notre Dame team. Joe said:

"I remember walking to the locker-room and wondering what Rock would say. We flopped down in the room and waited for him. We kept looking at the door but he never showed up. The three-minute warning signal rang and still no Rock. Finally, he walked in. He was really mad. 'The Fighting Irish,' he said, in a voice that curled your shoulder pads. 'Well, you'll be able to tell your grandchildren you're the first Notre Dame team that ever quit.' He turned to Hunk Anderson, his assistant coach, and said, 'You take 'em, Hunk. I'm through with them.' Then he walked out.

"I don't remember how we got through that door, but I remember that Rome Dugan was standing behind it, and he got flattened against the wall when we broke through it. We went out there and took the kickoff and slammed 75 yards for a touchdown. Didn't use a pass or an end run. Enright and Flanagan just socked through tackle and guard until we went over. When they kicked to us again, we pounded another 78 yards for another score. We won, 13 to 10.

"Earlier I looked over at the bench, and Rock was nowhere in sight. But by the end of the game, he was there, crouching on the sideline, twiddling that cigar, just as if nothing had happened."

Rock was a great believer in the power of words. He knew that the right word at the right time might do more for a lagging lineman than hours of sweat on the tackling dummy or the blocking machine. More often than not, the word stuck with the player and he will tell you he is a better man for it today. That is one good reason why the Rock transcended other football coaches. His methods for getting the most out of a player were varied and unpredictable. He could be soothingly gentle or brutally scornful. He practiced such ego-smashing stunts as playing the Four Horsemen in a practice scrimmage behind a third-string line, and then snapping at the star backfielders, "Show 'em your clippings, boys!"

When his players talk about Rockne's caustic tongue ("We never knew the meaning of the word 'sarcastic' until we played for Rock.") they tell you that he never bore a grudge. He could make you despise him on the practice field but he usually sent you back to the dorm admiring him. Old Notre Dame men have special memories of him. Moose Krause tells of his first meeting with Rockne in 1930 when he was a freshman. "I was just one of dozens of guys trying to make it at tackle," he says. "I was in awe of Rockne. When my folks came to South Bend to see me, the first thing they asked was would I introduce them to Rockne. Well, I was a little worried by the suggestion. I had no idea how to go about it. We were walking across the campus that day and who should come down the steps of the Main Building but Rock. I was wondering if I had the nerve to speak to him. He walked over to me and said, 'Moose, how are you getting along with the books?' You could have knocked me over. He even called me Moose. My folks were mighty impressed. So was I. I never forgot it."

Rockne's magnetism had many elements, as you find out when you talk to those who knew him best, but one of its essential ingredients was his humor. His players remember it as often, if not more often, as they remember his tongue-lashings. Rockne's humor was not saved for the speaker's platform or for interviews with the press. His wit bubbled over at the most unexpected times. Born a Norse Protestant, he was baptized as a Catholic in 1925 at the Log Chapel on the South Bend campus, a replica of Notre Dame's original first buildings. He noticed that only one candle was lit on the altar and asked about it. A priest explained that the baptism service called for only a single candle. The Rock said, "It seems to me you guys are awfully tight with the wax."

Many young people today assume that Rockne was an old man when he died in 1931. He was 43, just reaching his professional peak. He was born March 4, 1888, in Voss, Norway, the son of a renowned carriage maker who came to Chicago when one of his carriages was being exhibited there at a World's Fair. The Rockne family stayed on and settled in the Logan Square section of the city.

Knute Kenneth Rockne, or Rock or Swede, as he was called in the neighborhood, was a small, wiry youth with a somewhat unusual devotion to books who did better at track in high school than in football. He pole-vaulted and ran the middle-distances. Rock never finished high school. In March, 1907, he took a job as a clerk in the main Post Office in Chicago at $50 a month, working mostly at night and competing in track meets with Chicago athletic clubs. He remained at the postal clerk's job until Nobember, 1910, with his salary advancing to almost $100 a month. He was planning to enroll as a student at the University of Illinois but apparently two track pals, Johnny Plant and Johnny Devine, persuaded him to attend Notre Dame instead. Rock later wrote that his decision was made after they convinced him that he could live more cheaply in South Bend. He was admitted to the university in the fall of 1910 after passing the entrance examination with a high grade. Rock was more mature than his classmates, but even his advanced age does not account for the brilliant scholastic record that he made at Notre Dame. His scholastic average for four years was 92.5, more than enough for a *magna cum laude*. In ten of his subjects, he received a grade of 100, seven of those courses in sciences. His special forte was chemistry.

While winning varsity letters in track and football, Rockne edited his senior class's yearbook, made a name for himself as a comedian in dramatics, did a brief hitch as a flute player in the band, and helped pay for his board and room by waiting on dining room tables and working as a janitor. As left end of the Irish football team, Rockne caught forward passes thrown by the quarterback, Gus Dorais, who wrote in later years that he first saw Rock on the campus wearing corduroy pants held up by white suspenders, a blue jersey and a cap. A flattened nose, broken by a baseball bat in high school, and a balding head gave him an uncommonly rugged appearance for a college boy. Dorais said that Rock tried countless prescriptions to check his falling hair but none worked. Westbrook Pegler, the caustic columnist, once described Rock as having the appearance of "the old, punched-up preliminary fighter who becomes doortender in a speakeasy, and sits in a shadowy corner near the door at night, recalling the time he fought Billy Papke in Peoria for $50." Rockne never forgave Pegler for it, but it was an appropriate word picture.

As a football player at Notre Dame, Rockne's name in the minds of most people is connected with one game. That is the first Notre Dame–Army game in 1913. But he was stand-out All-American end long before that game.

It is also a popular myth that Notre Dame, before that Army game, was a tiny college in the Midwest with little football experience. Actually the Irish had won 26 games without a defeat since 1910. The victory over West Point in 1913 by the score of 35 to 13 naturally did much to promote Notre Dame in the East but the way the game was won caused more comment than the score. Army was done under by a passing attack that had never been seen in the East. The pass was not a revolutionary weapon at the time, but Notre Dame's use of it was.

Notre Dame had a 14–13 lead going into the last period. Then the passes thrown by Dorais to Rockne, Joe Pliska, Sam Finnegan, Fred Gurshurst and others brought repeated long gains that forced the Cadets to spread their defense wide. Dorais took advantage of the thinly spread line by sending Ray Eichenlaub, the All-American fullback, rushing through the guards and tackles. He cracked the line for two touchdowns; Rockne scored one of the others catching a pass. Most of the reporters at the game disagreed on the number of passes thrown and completed by the Irish. But accepted figures are 13 out of 17, for a total of 243 yards.

When Rockne graduated from Notre Dame in 1914, he wrestled with the idea of studying medicine. Instead he stayed on the campus to take on an instructorship in chemistry and to work as an assistant to Jess Harper, the football coach. Chet Grant, a quarterback on the Harper-Rockne 1916 squad, recalled later that the players looked to Jess for a tactical plan and to Rock for inspiration. "Even then, Rock was a first-class orator," Chet said. "He delivered some stirring pep talks. I'll never forget one he gave before the Wabash game. I don't know why he wasted such dramatic words on Wabash, but my feet tingled all the way to the field." Notre Dame won, 60 to 0.

Under Harper and Rockne, Notre Dame's pre–World War I football fortunes rose to the point of even getting a game with a Western Conference team, Wisconsin, ending a seven-year refusal by the Big Ten to recognize the Irish as a college worth speaking to on the gridiron. Among the Notre Dame players at that time was George Gipp. Harper and Rockne discovered Gipp when he was a freshman player on a dormitory team. The coaches first noticed his punting. Still a freshman, he got his name into the football record books by drop-kicking a 62-yard field goal against Purdue in 1916, but he was also a picture runner, one of those easy-does-it natural athletes who can always seem to rise to the occasion, extending himself to superhuman lengths when needed. Against Purdue in 1920, he went 80 and then 92 yards for touchdowns and in the Army game that fall he gained 332 yards rushing. Rockne appreciated Gipp's nimble brain and his ability to improvise under pressure. He was two plays ahead of everyone else on the field.

After the 1920 football season ended, Gipp and all of the other varsity lettermen attended a team banquet in the Oliver Hotel at South Bend. Half way through the dinner, he asked Chet Grant if he could borrow Chet's handkerchief. He took it and walked up to Rockne's chair and whispered something to the coach. Then he walked out. No one was worried about him or thought his absence unusual. Gipp was off to seek his own evening, that was all. A couple of days later, he was in bed with tonsillitis. Then he was taken to the hospital with pneumonia. While he was in the hospital, Walter Camp announced that he had picked Gipp on his first string All-America team, the first Notre Dame man so honored. Within a week, Gipp was dead, less than a month after he had played his last game for Notre Dame.

There is, of course, the famous sequel to the Gipp story. It is so stuffed with melodrama that it probably has become the most mangled of all the Rockne stories, as it was in the Pat O'Brien movie version of Rockne's life. People have understandably questioned its ever happening. Yet to understand Rockne it is important to know why and how it *did* happen. In 1928, Rockne had his poorest season at Notre Dame. The Irish lost four games that fall, one third of the number of all the games Rockne lost during his entire career as a head coach. It was not a bad team but it suffered some bad luck and some bad injuries. When Notre Dame went to New York to play Army, it was given little chance of winning. The Cadets had Chris Cagle in their backfield and a record of six victories.

In the Notre Dame locker room at Yankee Stadium before the game, Rockne delivered his most stirring fight talk. He told the squad about George Gipp, about his perfection on the football team, of his exceptional ability to come through when he was needed most, about his sudden illness and his death. He said that on his death bed Gipp made two requests. He asked, first, to become a Catholic and he asked that someday, when the odds were piled high against Notre Dame, he wished that Rock would ask the team to win one for him. Rockne told the story in a low, emotion-choked voice. When he finished, he said, "This is that game." The players sat, rubbing their hands and staring at the floor, their eyes filling with tears. Mayor Jimmy Walker of New York leaned against one wall of the locker room, blinking his eyes. Two New York policemen, standing at the door, wept unrestrainedly.

Notre Dame won the game, 12 to 6. If it takes the edge off the story to say that the touchdowns came in the second half and Rock's act was before the game began, it is nevertheless important to keep history straight. Often overlooked, too, is the fact that Army had punched its way to Notre Dame's one-yard line when the game ended. But the play of the Irish was wonderfully inspired. The first Notre Dame touchdown was made by Jack Chevigny, an emotional, do-or-die player. Chevigny slammed across from the one-yard line in the third period, tying the score, 6 to 6. As he picked himself up in the end zone he is supposed to have said, "That's one for the Gipper!"

The winning touchdown came spectacularly in the last quarter. With the ball in Notre Dame's possession on the Army 22 yard line, Rockne substituted Johnny O'Brien, a tall, willowy end, who was a fine hurdler on the track team but too slight for steady action in football. Quarterback Pat Brady called O'Brien's number on the next play. Bill Dew, replacing Chevigny at right half, took the pass from center, faked a run to his left and shoveled the ball to Butch Niemic, who also faked a run and then threw a long, arching pass to O'Brien behind Army's defensive left halfback. O'Brien juggled the ball as he raced for the end zone, finally clutching it to his chest as he fell over the line. Johnny, who was killed a few years later in a car crash, was known as "One Play" O'Brien after that.

That Army game will always be remembered as "The Gipp Game," but actually it was not the first time Rock pulled the Gipp story on one of his teams. In 1921, the year after Gipp died, Notre Dame met Indiana in Indianapolis. In a hotel room before the game, Rock spoke to the players, many of whom had played with George, and asked them to win one for the Gipper. Stuffed with emotion and incentive, they did, 28 to 7.

Playing one climactic act after another, Rockne, like any actor, had his bad shows. There weren't many, but he did boot a few. He read the wrong script before the 1922 Nebraska game. Before the team took the field at Lincoln, Rock was unusually quiet. But in the huddle on the field, he whipped out a telegram and read it to his team. It said that Notre Dame was being considered for the New Year's Day Rose Bowl game. Cod Cotton, a tackle on the team, says, "I went out there and all I saw was red roses, Gloria Swanson and Mary Pickford. Some of the other boys must have been affected the same way because we got beat, 13 to 7."

Two years later, Notre Dame, with the famous Four Horsemen, did play in the Rose Bowl, whipping Stanford, 27 to 10. It was Rockne's first and last bowl game.

That 1924 team gets vociferous support when Notre Dame men

argue about which squad was Rockne's greatest. The Four Horsemen were so dubbed by Grantland Rice as he watched them beat Army in the Polo Grounds. George Strickler, the student publicity agent at the time, was clever enough to see gold in the nickname, and he posed the backfield—Harry Stuhldreher, Jim Crowley, Don Miller and Elmer Layden—on horseback in their football uniforms for a picture that became one of the most widely reproduced sports photos of all time.

The Four Horsemen played together as a unit for the first time in 1922 against Carnegie Tech. Rockne brought them along so that by 1924 their special talents synchronized perfectly. The strength of this backfield lay in its machinelike precision. Each part fitted smoothly into the whole. It was a small backfield, averaging about 165 pounds, and it ran behind a relatively light line (inevitably called The Seven Mules), although tackles Rip Miller and Joe Bach, and center Adam Walsh, all weighed over 190.

In the Rose Bowl game against Stanford, Rock, typically, did not start the Four Horsemen. He sent in his second backfield and let his famous heroes sit on the bench until well into the first period. When they were put into the game, they were ready to tear Stanford apart.

Notre Dame became so famous for its smart offensive football that there is a tendency to overlook Rock's defensive genius. Jack Lavelle, a Notre Dame graduate who was one of the best known football scouts, contended that Rockne was the finest defensive coach the game has ever seen. No winning score of more than 27 points was ever posted against Rockne. He once said jokingly, "I like my guards and tackles dumb and strong." Actually, he would not tolerate a dumb lineman.

Rockne made so few misjudgments on his own players and on opposing teams that when he did blunder, the story was splashed across newspapers everywhere. In 1926, the Irish were heading toward another undefeated and untied season record, having bowled over their first eight opponents. Their last game was against Carnegie Tech on November 27 at Pittsburgh. On the same day, at Soldiers Field in Chicago, Army was playing Navy. Rock decided to turn his team over to Hunk Anderson, his assistant, and went to Chicago. He wanted to get a look at Navy because the Annapolis team was to be on Notre Dame's schedule for the first time in the following year's season. Carnegie Tech had lost to Washington and Jefferson and to New York University, and had just beaten John Carroll, 7 to 0.

While Rockne sat in the press box at Soldiers Field, Notre Dame lost to Carnegie Tech in Pittsburgh, 13 to 0. Rock was buried under wires from indignant alumni, demanding to know what he was doing in Chicago while his team was getting beaten in Pittsburgh. He offered no alibi. Two years later, on the Saturday following the famous "Gipp Game" win over Army, Notre Dame met Carnegie Tech again. Whipped to an emotional frenzy in the Army game the week before, the Notre Dame team was not up for this one. Tech, led by its classy all-around star, Howard Harpster, scored a 27 to 7 victory.

This serves as background for one of the most dramatic locker-room scenes in Rockne's career. In 1929, he suffered severely from phlebitis and a serious bloodclot developed in one of his legs. In the fall of that year, Tom Lieb and other assistants had to do most of the active coaching work. Rockne was occasionally reduced to sitting on the sidelines in a wheelchair, shouting orders through a megaphone.

During the week before the Carnegie Tech game, Rock was flat on his back under doctor's orders. He was forbidden to make the trip to Pittsburgh, but he persuaded his doctor to accompany him to the game. When he arrived at the stadium, he asked Tom Lieb to carry him into the locker room. Francis Wallace, a close friend of Rockne's and a Chicago sportswriter, was in the room that afternoon. He described the scene in his book, *The Notre Dame Story*. Rockne, placed on a table by Lieb, leaned his back on a wall, his bad leg stretched out in front of him. He sat for a long time, facing the players, saying nothing. His face was pale and drawn. His doctor, Maurice Keady, leaned over to Wallace and whispered, "He has an even chance of not leaving this room alive. If that clot is loosened from the excitement it could kill him."

Finally, Rockne spoke and these are his words as recalled by Wallace: "There has been a lot of water under the bridge since I first came to Notre Dame—but I don't know when I wanted to win a game as badly as this one. I don't care what happens after today. Why do you think I am taking a chance like this, coming here? To see you lose?" His voice rose. "They'll be primed. They'll be tough. They think they have your number. Are you going to let it happen to you again? You can win if you want to!"

Then he poured it on in that loud, sharp staccato:

"Go out there and hit 'em! Crack 'em! Crack 'em! Fight to live! Fight to win! Fight to win . . . win . . . . win . . . WIN!" The door banged open, and the players, many of them in tears, clattered to their feet and pushed their way out of the room.

Would you swallow that scene in a Hollywood movie? Probably not. But it happened. You could, of course, charge Rockne with making a maudlin spectacle of his own illness, playing too loosely with the emotions of a bunch of kids. But Rockne himself was choked with emotion that afternoon. He apparently didn't know how long he was going to live. And he wanted to beat Carnegie Tech. He did. Joe Savoldi punched his way through the Carnegie line in the third period for the only score of the game. Notre Dame won all of the other games on its schedule, defeating Southern California, 13 to 12, on the final Saturday. Rockne supervised that one from a wheelchair, too.

The climax of Rockne's life came in the next year, 1930. It had a rare fictional quality, too. The 1930 squad, in the estimation of many people, was the finest ever assembled by Rockne. In the backfield were Frank Carideo at quarterback, Marchy Schwartz and Marty Brill as halfbacks and Jumping Joe Savoldi and Larry (Moon) Mullins alternating at fullback. There was another shifty halfback available, Paul (Bucky) O'Connor. In the line were such All-Americas as Bert Metzger at guard, center Tommy Yarr, tackle Joe Kurth and guard Nordy Hoffman.

In the opening game of the season, Joe Savoldi returned a Southern Methodist kickoff 98 yards for a touchdown and the Irish won by a score of 20 to 14. Then they defeated Drake (28–7), Indiana (27–0), Northwestern (14–0), Pittsburgh (35–19), Carnegie Tech (21–6), Navy (26–2), Army (7–6) and Pennsylvania (60–20). The big final game of the season was to be with Southern California, a team that had beaten Stanford, 42 to 12, California, 74 to 0, and U.C.L.A., 52 to 0. The week before the Southern California game, Joe Savoldi, the star Notre Dame fullback, got himself kicked out of college. Joe not only had gotten married, which was against the university's rules at that time, but he got divorced, which was against the university's religion.

Not only was Rock without Savoldi. His other star fullback, Moon Mullins, who usually started the games in that position, had a lame leg and was not ready to play. Rockne worked out a scheme at Tucson where Notre Dame practiced on Thursday before resuming their train trip to California for the big game on Saturday. Dan Hanley, the third string fullback, lacked real experience, so Rock decided to use the speedy and elusive Bucky O'Connor, a halfback, in the fullback position. He also decided that Southern California had better not know about this change in the line-up. He would have O'Connor wear Hanley's jersey and number, and vice-versa.

"Can you imagine," Frank Leahy said later, "a coach doing that today? Rockne was the only guy who could get away with it."

O'Connor, posing as Hanley, worked out at fullback in a practice session before the eyes of a group of Los Angeles newspapermen. He ran short bucks, as Hanley would, and did none of the wide outside running at which he excelled. Posing as Hanley, he was interviewed by a Los Angeles sports columnist.

The plan worked. Ninety thousand people in the Los Angeles Coliseum saw Notre Dame dismantle the Trojans. Schwartz fired a pass to Carideo for the first touchdown. Then, on a reverse, Brill tossed a lateral to Bucky O'Connor who was wheeling around end, and Bucky went 80 yards to score. A lateral pass from Schwartz shook Bucky loose again later in the game and he went seven yards for the third touchdown. The final score was 27 to 0.

In legends, the hero's life is snuffed out immediately after he has made his greatest conquest, at the very summit of his career. And so it was with Rockne. Cynics say that the Rockne myth has been enhanced by the fact that the man never reached the point of backslide, that had he lived longer, time would have caught up with him. All we know for certain is that Rockne was still far out in front when he died.

A winter trip to Florida and the prospect of another fine team at Notre Dame in 1931 had a salubrious effect on Rockne's health. In March, 1931, he planned a trip to Los Angeles by plane to confer with directors of a series of movie shorts. The night before he left Chicago on the flight to the Coast, he ate dinner with Christy Walsh, his friend and business partner, and Albert C. Fuller, a local hotel man. When he got into the cab, Fuller said to him, "Soft landings, coach."

"You mean happy landings, don't you?" Rock said.

The next day, March 31, 1931, the passenger plane carrying Rockne and seven other people exploded in the air and crashed in a pasture near Bazaar, Kansas. There were no survivors.

The rare influence that Knute Rockne had on so many people, and on the game of football itself, can still be felt when you talk about him with people who were close to him. One of them, a prominent professional man in Cleveland, says, "It is hard to understand the impact he had on us. Do you know that not a single night since he died, not once, have I gone to bed without saying a prayer for the Swede?"

Talk to those who knew Rockne best and you agree with Father John W. Cavanaugh, a past president of Notre Dame, when he says, "I think that you will find, after all, that the man is greater than the legend."

# Louis Knocks Out Schmeling

## *Bob Considine*

The evening of June 22, 1938, was a big night in the life of Joe
Louis, the youngest world heavyweight champion in history.
Two years earlier, Max Schmeling, the German Nazi apostle of
white Aryan supremacy, had knocked out the Brown Bomber
from Detroit in the twelfth round of their first fight at Yankee
Stadium, giving the highly favored Louis the only defeat in his
career up to that time. Joe had gone on to win the heavyweight
title from Jim Braddock a year later, at the age of twenty-three,
and now, in 1938, he was back in the ring at the Stadium, facing
Schmeling once again. Here is Bob Considine at the ringside
telling you what happened next.

Listen to this, buddy, for it comes from a guy whose palms are still
wet, whose throat is still dry, and whose jaw is still agape from the
utter shock of watching Joe Louis knock out Max Schmeling.

It was a shocking thing, that knockout—short, sharp, merciless,
complete. Louis was like this:

He was a big lean copper spring, tightened and retightened
through weeks of training until he was one pregnant package of
coiled venom.

Schmeling hit that spring. He hit it with a whistling right-hand
punch in the first minute of the fight—and the spring, tormented
with tension, suddenly burst with one brazen spang of activity.
Hard brown arms, propelling two unerring fists, blurred beneath

the hot white candelabra of the ring lights. And Schmeling was in the path of them, a man caught and mangled in the whirring claws of a mad and feverish machine.

The mob, biggest and most prosperous ever to see a fight in a ball yard, knew that there was the end before the thing had really started. It knew, so it stood up and howled one long shriek. People who had paid as much as $100 for their chairs didn't use them—except perhaps to stand on, the better to let the sight burn forever in their memories.

There were four steps to Schmeling's knockout. A few seconds after he landed his only punch of the fight, Louis caught him with a lethal little left hook that drove him into the ropes so that his right arm was hooked over the top strand, like a drunk hanging to a fence. Louis swarmed over him and hit with everything he had —until Referee Donovan pushed him away and counted one.

Schmeling staggered away from the ropes, dazed and sick. He looked drunkenly toward his corner, and before he had turned his head back Louis was on him again, first with a left and then that awe-provoking right that made a crunching sound when it hit the German's jaw. Max fell down, hurt and giddy, for a count of three.

He clawed his way up as if the night air were as thick as black water, and Louis—his nostrils like the mouth of a double-barreled shotgun—took a quiet lead and let him have both barrels.

Max fell almost lightly, bereft of his senses, his fingers touching the canvas like a comical stew-bum doing his morning exercises, knees bent and the tongue lolling in his head.

He got up long enough to be knocked down again, this time with his dark unshaven face pushed in the sharp gravel of the resin.

Louis jumped away lightly, a bright and pleased look in his eyes, and as he did the white towel of surrender which Louis' handlers had refused to use two years ago tonight came sailing into the ring in a soggy mess. It was thrown by Max Machon, oblivious to the fact that fights cannot end this way in New York.

The referee snatched it off the floor and flung it backwards. It hit the ropes and hung there, limp as Schmeling. Donovan counted up to five over Max, sensed the futility of it all, and stopped the fight.

The big crowd began to rustle restlessly toward the exits, many only now accepting Louis as champion of the world. There were no eyes for Schmeling, sprawled on his stool in his corner.

He got up eventually, his dirty gray-and-black robe over his shoulders, and wormed through the happy little crowd that hovered around Louis. And he put his arm around the Negro and smiled. They both smiled and could afford to—for Louis had made around $200,000 a minute and Schmeling $100,000 a minute.

But once he crawled down in the belly of the big stadium, Schmeling realized the implications of his defeat. He, who won the title on a partly phony foul, and beat Louis two years ago with the aid of a crushing punch after the bell had sounded, now said Louis had fouled him. That would read better in Germany, whence earlier in the day had come a cable from Hitler, calling on him to win.

It was a low, sneaking trick, but a rather typical last word from Schmeling.

# The Haig

## John Lardner

Maybe Walter Hagen was not quite the greatest golfer who ever lived, but he was the most colorful personality in the history of the game. One day when Johnny Farrell was winning a big tournament with no spectators following him, another player said to him, "Where's the crowd?" Farrell said, "Over behind the caddie house, watching Hagen play mumblety-peg." John Lardner, who was Robert Frost's favorite sportswriter, composed this tribute to Hagen shortly before his own death in 1959 at the age of forty-seven. Ten years later, when The Haig died, his philosophy of life was inscribed on his casket: "Don't hurry. Don't worry. You're only here on a short visit, so don't forget to stop and smell the flowers."

Once, a man named Walter Hagen had a date to play a morning round of golf in Tokyo with Prince Konoye, of the royal blood of Japan. Hagen appeared at the clubhouse at noon.

"The Prince has been waiting since ten o'clock," he was told.

"Well," said Hagen, "he wasn't going anywhere, was he?"

There you hear the voice of one who succeeded, as few members of our meekly desperate species have done, in adjusting the shape, speed and social laws of the world to his own tastes. Hagen was especially fearless of time; and, maybe for that reason, time has been respectful to Hagen. It's now more than a dozen years since the Haig quit playing even friendly golf. (It was no fun any more; the finest putting touch in the history of the game had been fatally marred by, he said, a "whisky jerk.")

That's a long while to be out of action, out of the hot news, and still to be constantly remembered. But Hagen, rusticating in a house on a hill by a lake in Michigan where the water is cold enough to chase Scotch without ice, remains a living force in sport. They still talk about him with an awe and wonder as fresh as in the days when he had the golf world in a bottle, as the old song goes, and the stopper in his hand.

"Golf never had a showman like him," Gene Sarazen said two or three years ago. "All the professionals who have a chance to go after the big money today should say a silent thanks to Walter Hagen each time they stretch a check between their fingers. It was Hagen who made professional golf what it is."

By land and sea, in airplanes and in Wall Street, the age of Walter Hagen was the age of gorgeous individualism and golden soloists. In sports, the champions were Ruth, Dempsey, Tilden, Jones, Grange—and this fellow with sleek black hair, a full-moon face, and hooded, oddly oriental eyes, who dressed himself to shine like the Milky Way on a clear night, and who used to say, by way of explaining how life should be lived: "Don't hurry. Don't worry. You're only here on a short visit, so don't forget to stop and smell the flowers."

Seemingly, Hagen lived by that rule. In earning more than a million dollars at golf, he spent money as fast as he made it and often a little faster. Once, after winning the Canadian Open, he wired ahead to a Montreal hotel, as the first step in a victory party: "Fill one bathtub with champagne." The cost of the party eventually came to $200 more than the prize money he'd won in the tournament.

But, like other things about Hagen, the gay, hedonistic code was deceptive. If he had the philosophy of a butterfly and the appetites of a Pasha, he had a brain like a pair of barber's shears.

In fact, he was full of contradictions:

1. "In swinging," said Mike King Brady, the old pro who first took him on the road in 1914, "Hagen sways like a rocking horse."

But, says Ben Hogan, in speaking of golf technique, there is a fundamental kind of rhythm which "could also be described as the order of procedure. Walter Hagen was probably the greatest exponent of this kind of rhythm ever to play golf."

2. Hagen was prodigal with cash, a high spender and tipper, a compulsive check-grabber, a plunger on long, bright motor cars and soft, bright clothing.

But—he took care years ago to fix things so that he lives in perfect security today, on royalties and commissions from golf equipment.

3. Hagen was a loner and an egotist at golf, a pitiless competitor. He used every trick in the book of psychology to trim his friends and fellow pros.

But—he raised the living standards and promoted the independence of all professional athletes as did no one else, even Babe Ruth. By sheer force of his own love of comfort and freedom, he carried his profession onward and upward on his back. He revolutionized the status of the golf pro—from janitor to social hero.

Hagen's first job as a club pro, in 1912, paid him $1,200 for eight months, and this was not unusual. For several years after that, few pros averaged better than $50 a week. Socially, club members treated them in a friendly but patronizing way, like a chauffeur or a valuable cook. In 1914, $75 was a pro's standard charge for an exhibition match. By 1915, Hagen was asking and getting $200 and $300 for an exhibition, and he was mixing freely with millionaires and needling them into $500 nassaus in private games. They took it and loved it. By the time he had planted his full, democratic, do-it-my-way-or-to-hell-with-you brand on golf and on society, the American pro was a big shot, with a limitless earning capacity—and the European pro had come out of the servants' entrance and knew himself to be a man, as good as his talent could make him.

4. Hagen was a party guy, a night-bird, a wrecker of training rules.

But—he was also a sure-handed, clear-eyed all-around athlete, a winner at the top level for 30 years. (He won the croquet championship of Florida in his first try at the game. And once he out-shot the whole field at a national live-bird shooting tournament.) Hagen didn't smoke or drink till he was 26. Then he became a chain-smoker, and went on winning. And when he discovered prohibition liquor, his luck stayed with him. It turned out that the man had a head like an old oaken bucket.

Take a look at him early on a hot summer morning in 1926. A golf fan stood in front of the Garden City Hotel on Long Island, admiring the dawn and thinking what a fine day it would be for the final round of the national PGA championship, when he noticed a dapper figure in a tuxedo approaching the hotel from out of the sunrise. It was Hagen—scheduled that afternoon to play Leo Diegel for the highest prize in professional golf. He had been training for the match by making a tour of Manhattan speakeasies. "Good morning," said Hagen civilly.

"Good morning," said the startled fan. "Do you know that Diegel has been in bed since ten o'clock last night?"

"Maybe he has been in bed," said Hagen, as he walked on into the hotel. "But he hasn't been sleeping."

That was an accurate analysis—not only of Diegel, but of all Hagen opponents. A few hours later, Hagen won the championship by a score of 5 and 3, the third of his four consecutive PGA match play titles.

The game with Diegel was one of a string of 29 PGA matches in a row that Hagen won, over a period of five years, from the best and smartest golfers in the world. In his time, he captured 11 national American and British titles, including the British Open four times and the U.S. Open twice. When he gave up the game at the age of 50, he had, in fact, proved everything.

Was he the greatest? His fellow pros said so in 1938, when they voted for him by two to one over Bobby Jones as the greatest tournament golfer they had ever seen. But "great" and "greatest" have become loose, flabby words in the sporting vocabulary. There were some who tried to describe Hagen more exactly, by calling him "the world's best bad golfer." Bob Jones himself once expressed the special, mortifying essence of Hagen even better, in something he said a few years ago, during the heyday of Ben Hogan.

In a way, Jones observed, a steady, consistent, mechanized

player like Hogan makes an "easy" opponent at golf. Nothing he does surprises you; you can focus your mind on your own work. "But," Jones said, "when the other fellow misses his drive, and then misses his second shot, and then beats you out of the hole with a birdie, it gets your goat!"

He was speaking of Hagen—and Hagen had an answer to every criticism of this kind in one of his maxims: "The object of the game is to get the ball into the hole."

"Get your goat" is a gentle way of stating what Hagen did to Jones in a 72-hole match they played in Florida in 1926 for "the championship of the world" (and also, as will be noted again later, for the purpose of selling real estate). Hagen went from stump to bush to sand, and, in the end, beat Jones by the whopping margin of 12 and 11. His purse, the biggest ever paid a golfer for one match, was $7,600. Off the top of this sum, he peeled $800, and bought Jones a pair of diamond-and-platinum cufflinks.

"We must encourage the breed of amateur," Hagen explained sweetly. "They draw their share of the customers, and we take their share of the gravy."

So saying, he leaped aboard his Madame X Cadillac (a deluxe model of the period, of which Hagen owned the first specimen ever produced), and rode to his office to see how things were doing in the business (Florida golf promotion) which at that time paid him $30,000 a year and included, among other things, a blonde secretary who played the ukulele. The automobile was the latest in a line of flamboyant, Hagen-bearing vehicles that went well back into motor car history: a Chalmers, a Stephens-Duryea, a Chandler with an orange-and-black check, a red Lozier, a Pierce-Arrow, and in England, chartered Rolls-Royces and Austin-Daimlers.

This was the good life—the life toward which the Haig had begun to move a long time before, on the spring day when he climbed out the window of his seventh-grade classroom in Rochester, never to return to the field of formal education; at least, not regularly.

The schoolroom window commanded an irresistible view of the

country club of Rochester. There, Hagen had first broken 80 in the year 1904, at the age of 11. As a caddie at the country club, he made 10 cents an hour, plus tips. His father, William Hagen, as a blacksmith in the railroad-car shops, made $18 a week. Once the younger Hagen had put the distractions of school behind him, he passed his father economically. A little later, he passed Andy Christy, the club pro, artistically. It cannot be said that Christy enjoyed this. In 1912, Andy went to the National Open in Buffalo with another pro, and took Hagen, who had become his assistant, along. In a practice round, Hagen shot the course in 73.

"I'm thinking," said Christy, who was shooting much higher, "that someone should be home minding the shop. You can catch a train at 5:45."

The quick trip to Buffalo was not, however, a complete blank for Hagen; a whole new world was unfolded to him there. He was struck half blind with inspiration by the sight of a golfer named Tom Anderson, who wore a white silk shirt with blue, red, black and yellow stripes, white flannel pants, a red bandanna around his neck, a loud plaid cap, and white buckskin shoes with wide laces and red soles.

By the time of the 1913 Open, at Brookline, Massachusetts, Hagen had reproduced the entire costume for his own use, except that he replaced the bandanna with an Ascot tie imported from London. This conservative touch was to be typical of his own evolving taste in clothes-horsemanship. He became a rainbow, but a smooth, sophisticated rainbow.

The 1913 U.S. Open at Brookline, which Hagen played in candy-striped shirt and red-soled shoes, was his first big tournament. It is famous today for the playoff in which a young American named Francis Ouimet beat out the British masters Vardon and Ray; few remember that Hagen finished behind those three, narrowly missing the playoff. The next year, at 21, he took the title, tying the tournament record with 290.

The win was crucial—it saved Hagen from becoming a Philadelphia Phillie. The Phils had tried him out both as a right-handed pitcher and as a left-hand-hitting outfielder. Having tasted top money in golf, Hagen evaded their snares. The signs of ambidexterity, however, stayed with him for life. There was no right-hander in golf who could play the rare and occasionally vital left-handed shot better, from a tree or a wall or a water bank. Sometimes Hagen played it with a putter or the heel of a right-handed iron, sometimes with a left-handed club he carried for emergencies.

He had 85 other ways of beating you, as the pros of the old balloon-ball era discovered. The pros were, in the main, a dour, cautious, Scotsmanly lot. Once, in Florida, on the morning of a one-day $500 tournament, a group of them agreed to eliminate cabfare by accepting Hagen's invitation to drive them to the course in his new open-top car. Hagen appeared at the rendezvous a half hour late. "We must go like hell, men!" he cried, with a look at his watch. They did. It was several months before they recovered fully from the ride. Hagen won the $500.

The Al Jolson musical show *Sinbad* was playing Boston in 1919 at the time Hagen acquired his second U.S. Open title, at the Brae Burn course near there. Hagen had recently learned how to oil his metabolism with occasional "hoots." ("Hoot" was one of his favorite words for a drink of whisky. Another was "hyposonica.") He saw a good deal of the Jolson troupe, after showtime, during the tournament. A gala getaway party was arranged for the night following the last round of the Open. As things turned out, the last round left Hagen tied for first place with Mike Brady. This called for a playoff next day, but Hagen did not see his way clear to passing up the party.

In the dawn that followed the revels, he left the flower and the chivalry of *Sinbad*, took a shower at his hotel, proceeded to the course by Pierce-Arrow, had two quick double Scotches in the clubhouse bar, and joined Brady at the first tee. Hagen, who did not feel entirely in the pink, decided that a dose of strategy was in order. Brady, prepared to do a man's work, had his shirt sleeves rolled well up toward the shoulders. "Listen, Mike," said Hagen,

as they reached the second tee, "hadn't you better roll down those
sleeves?" "What for?" Brady asked. "The gallery can see your
muscles twitching," Hagen said. Brady hooked his tee shot violently, and lost the hole by two strokes. Hagen's margin at the end,
as he won the championship again, was one stroke.

This, it should be noted, was medal play. Hagen's favorite style
was match play, in which he could bring all the resources of his
erratic long game, his murderous pitching and putting, his aggressive coolness, his concentration, and his sharp personal tactics to
bear against one man. In the medal style of the open game, he was
never happier than when he could reduce a tournament to man-
to-man combat. The record shows—and it shows it of no one else
in history—that in 30 years of big-league golf, Hagen never lost a
playoff.

In private golf, in exhibitions, he tried always to introduce the
personal element, the head-on gambling touch, that brought out
his best. After the First World War, Hagen became the first
important professional golfer to cut loose completely from the
normal pro's life, a shop-and-lessons contract with a single country
club. This led to endless exhibition tours. On tour, he always
reached for the extra gamble.

At one strange club, he heard that the course record was 67, and
offered to bet he would tie it. A member of the reception committee was willing to stake $50 against him. "Well," Hagen said, "the
sun is high, and we have lots of time. Maybe we can do better
than fifty." Eventually, a pool of $3,000 was raised among mem-
bers, which Hagen faded.

The membership then followed Hagen around the course in a
body. On the last green, he needed to sink a 12-foot putt to tie the
record. He tapped the ball, and yelled, "Pay me, suckers!" before
it dropped. It dropped.

A time was to arrive, and soon, when Hagen came to consider
the British Open—especially on the seaside courses, lashed by
wind and rain, with their shaggy rough and bony greens—as the
truest test in golf, and a nagging challenge to himself personally.

He was the first American-born golfer to win the British championship, at Deal in 1922. Before that, before he learned to throw away the effete book of American golf, with its high driving, pitching, and exploding, and its controllable greens, and to master the British technique of the low shot and the pitch-and-run, he was tossed back violently on the seat of his pants. On his first trip abroad, in 1920, British golf overpowered Hagen.

His playing partner on the last round was a civil old gentleman of 62, who became the only player Hagen beat in the tournament. The old gentleman finished 54th, Hagen 53rd. The American champion's golf gave the British many a dry chuckle. But Hagen startled the press by obtaining a printed retraction of one slightly nasty piece by the simple but unprecedented method of telephoning the paper's owner, Lord Northcliffe. Hagen followed this step by carrying the social revolution to France—a traditional spot for revolutions.

He traveled to the French Open at La Boulie, near Paris, with the British stars George Duncan and Abe Mitchell. The dressing room for pros was a stable, with nails for the players' clothes and stalls for the livestock. "If they don't let us use the clubhouse," Hagen told Duncan and Mitchell, appointing himself chairman of a committee of three, "we will pull out."

The British pros, limp with class consciousness, followed him into the president's office. The president finally yielded the point—though the three foreigners were the only ones to get into the clubhouse. Hagen won the tournament in a playoff with the French champion Eugene Lafitte.

Within the next few years, as the Haig made Europe and England his playground and the British Open title almost his private property, the force of his golf and his brash and gaudy independence knocked over the remaining social barriers one by one. Britain was shaken by a habit Hagen had of using first-prize money in the Open (it ran to about $300) to tip his caddie with.

The Prince of Wales, later the Duke of Windsor, followed Hagen around when he played, and automatically picked locks for him socially. (There's a story that on a green in Bermuda, Hagen once said to the Duke, "Hold the pin, Eddie." This is apocryphal, according to Hagen. "What I told him was, 'Hold the pin, caddie.' ")

And while he removed the shackles from his fellow tradesmen, the Haig went on stealing their shirts and watches on the field of play. At La Boulie in 1920, striking a blow for liberty in France, he also ran Lafitte, his playoff opponent, dizzy. Hagen had heard that Lafitte hated to hurry his game. Hagen practically galloped around the course. At one hole, he climbed an uphill tee and drove before Lafitte had reached the top. Lafitte, panting after him, hurried his shot, and drove into the rough. The Frenchman lost his playoff by four strokes.

On the way to the playoff, Hagen used one of his favorite dodges, the wrong-club feint, to shake off Abe Mitchell. On a long hole, with his drive slightly ahead of Mitchell's, Hagen took his brassie from the bag as though to use it on the next shot. Big Abe went for the brassie too, and banged his ball into a row of trees that crossed the fairway. The Haig at once switched to his 2-iron, and hooked around the trees to a point just short of the green. The stroke he gained on this hole shut the Englishman out of the playoff.

The same ruse tricked Al Watrous out of a vital hole one day in the PGA. Hagen's tee shot fetched up against the foot of a tree. He saw where it went, but Watrous didn't. "You're away, Al," Hagen said, nonchalantly hefting his brassie. Watrous could see Hagen's club, if not Hagen's ball. He grabbed his own brassie, though what he needed was a control club for a deliberate slice. His ball bounced off a tree and into a brook. Hagen swiftly replaced the wood with a niblick, backhanded his own ball out of trouble, and won the hole and match.

It was a finesse, too, that started Bobby Jones off to disaster in their great "world championship" match in Florida in 1926. The first hole was a par 4. All its nastiness lay just beyond the green. Hagen, for his second shot, ostentatiously chose a 4-iron, and hit the ball a little softly—on purpose, critics have said. He landed short of the green. Jones, noting the shortness, used a 2-iron, overshot the carpet, had to struggle back, and lost the hole. From there on, Hagen never looked back as he marched to glory and a bag of gold and rubbed the great amateur's nose in the dirt.

It was heavily inflated dirt. The Florida land boom was on, and both Jones and Hagen had an interest in it. Hagen was president of the Pasadena Golf Club at St. Petersburg at $30,000 a year (plus a bonus of a couple of "hot lots"). Friends of the Jones family were anxious to glorify the real estate at Sarasota, down the line. The match consisted of 36 holes of golf at Jones's course, Sarasota, and 36 more a week later at Hagen's course. The region was crawling with butter-and-egg men, promoters, suckers, and other golf fans, and the air was charged with the rich flavor of gambling and excitement that Hagen loved.

The two players were clearly the world's best: Jones was American amateur and past Open champion, Hagen held the PGA and British Open titles.

Hagen took only 53 putts for the first 36 holes, and was 8 up at the end of them. On one green, after their second shots, Jones lay 40 feet from the cup and Hagen 20. Jones, using painstaking care, sank the ball—his finest putt of the match. "Whaddya know," shouted Hagen gaily, "he gets a half!" And while the meaning of these words was just coming home to his victim, he holed his own 20-footer with a quick slap. It was a gesture that Jones never forgot.

In the second half of their Florida "world series," the Hagen-Jones match went downhill in a rout. It ended at the 25th green. In one history-making stretch of 9 holes, Hagen needed only 7 putts—he got by on 7 long ones and 2 chip-ins. If the feat has ever been equalled, it was not done in the glare of the spotlight that bathed Hagen that day. The Haig agreed with other experts, as a general thing, that he always played his best golf with the 7- and 8-irons and the putter—the quick-death shots that can wipe out all past sins and break an opponent's heart. "I expect to make seven mistakes a round," Hagen used to say. "I always do. Why worry when I make them?" The short game always bailed him out.

He had an artist's passion for putting, and an engineer's skill at judging the roll and grain of a green. There was a putt in the PGA in 1925 that stopped Leo Diegel as though he had been shot with a gun. Diegel had Hagen 2 down with 2 to go in their quarter-final match. A 40-foot putt gave Diegel a 4 for the seventeenth hole; Hagen's second shot had left him 15 feet to the left of the cup on a fast downhill green with a double roll. Hagen plotted the putt with the help of a small leaf that lay uphill from the hole to the right. The ball had to stop at the leaf, catch the momentum of the green there, and roll downhill at an angle to find the cup. It did all of that. As it dropped, Diegel fell flat on his face on the green. Hagen won the next hole easily, squaring the match, and ended it on the fourth extra hole. Or, it might be said, he won it on the third extra hole. There, an intricate putt put Hagen down in 4. Diegel had a curving 30-inch putt to tie. It was a tricky one, as both men knew in their hearts. Suddenly, Hagen knocked Diegel's ball aside. "I'll give you that one, Leo," he said. "Let's play another hole." The surprise of the gesture wrecked what was left of Diegel's nerves. Overwrought, he blooped his next drive into a hayfield, and Hagen marched grandly on to the title.

Though he gave up normal pro-shop duties when he was 26, Hagen was a master club-maker and club-valet. Back in his early days, to earn a few extra dollars, he had worked as a mandolin-maker, and as a wood finisher in a piano factory. However, he had never made mandolins or finished pianos in the deep south, where conditions are a little different. In Florida, in the 1920's, the Haig launched a golf club factory that he figured would make him rich for life. In a round-about way it did. The clubs he produced were like poems by Keats—in Florida. When they were shipped north, however, the colder weather warped and shrank their shafts till they rattled like a spoon in a cup of coffee.

Hagen was in the red for $200,000 at the point where another rich friend, L. A. Young, Detroit's leading auto spring tycoon, put up his bail. The plant was shifted to Michigan. Under Young's management, and later under the Wilson Co.'s, it has provided the royalties that have kept Hagen in comfort, bright plumage, fast cars, and "hoots" for the rest of his life.

The adventure proved what every golf pro in the world came to be convinced of in time: that you cannot top a man who has God and the angels on his side. At the Inwood course, where he won his first PGA title in 1921, Hagen liked to play the seventeenth hole by driving down the eighteenth fairway—it gave him a more open shot at the green. During the night after the first round of the PGA, Jock Mackie, the home pro, with the backing of a group of local comedians, set up a big willow tree between the two fairways in such a position as to block Hagen's drive. The sudden sight of the tree, as he teed up his ball, gave the Haig a start. At almost the same moment, a gust of wind shook loose the tree's wiring and knocked the willow over on its side. "Excellent timing," said Hagen smugly, and made his usual drive.

Even the spectators, as time went on, became infected by a sense of the fellow's omnipotence. There was a one-day tournament at Catalina Island, in the 1920's, for which Hagen showed up late—he had been shooting goats in the mountains all morning with William Wrigley, the island's owner. Hagen raced around the course to finish before dark. With three holes to go, he learned of a low score by Horton Smith which led the field at the moment, with everyone in but Hagen. Seeing Smith in the gallery, Hagen called out genially, "Well, kid, I can tie you with a 3-2-1!" He got the 3, then got the 2, and then announced to the crowd, winking one inscrutable eye, "Now for the hole-in-one!" The hole was 190 yards. Hagen's tee shot hit the flag gently and stopped a foot from the cup.

Few mortal men can call a hole-in-one. And yet, Hagen once bet $10 even money at a short hole, in an exhibition match, that he would sink his tee shot, and then sank it. "The idea, when betting even money on a 100,000-to-1 shot," Hagen said mysteriously, as he pocketed the sawbuck, "is to recognize the one time when it comes along. It is done by clean living."

As noted, the U.S. PGA tournament was Hagen's special oyster for five straight years. It had to be. A cup went to the winner—and Hagen, unknown to everyone, had mislaid the cup. The name of this object was the Rodman Wanamaker Trophy, valued at $1,500. One day in 1925, Hagen, the temporary owner, left it in a taxicab in New York. He was always careless with silver. In 1926, he won the championship again. "You already have the Cup, Walter," the officials told him, "so keep it."

The same thing happened in 1927. In 1928, however, the patient Leo Diegel broke through and won the title. Hagen was asked to turn over the cup. "Well, I would like to," he said, "but I haven't got the slightest idea where it is." The pros themselves saved the situation by chipping in for another cup for Diegel.

Hazy or not as to certain kinds of detail, the old brain continued to perform like a shears, in one way, and like an oaken bucket, in another, as the Haig's golfing years drew to an end. They tell of a day in Belleair, Florida, in the West Coast Open, which followed a long, hard night. Hagen groped his way to the course, and took three practice shots. He topped a spoon shot, which traveled 40 feet. He topped a 2-iron shot, which traveled 20 feet. He topped a 5-iron shot, which traveled 6 feet. "Okay, I'm ready to play," Hagen said. He toured the course in 62.

And the Haig himself tells in his breezy book, *The Walter Hagen Story,* of another morning-after when his practice shots did the same kind of tricks, and the bright sun cut into his eyeballs like a knife. It was in Tampa, in 1935, when Hagen was 42. With a final hooker of corn liquor in him, he moved out from the soothing shadows of the locker room into the shimmering heat of the morning. Near the first tee, he saw three old friends from the Philadelphia Athletics ball club, Jimmy Foxx, Mickey Cochrane and Cy Perkins, waiting with the gallery to watch him tee off in the tournament. Hagen tottered over to them and shook their hands with loving enthusiasm. "Hiya, Jimmy. Hiya, Mike. Hiya, Cy," he said. "Haven't seen you in a hell of a long time." "Good luck, Haig," said Mr. Foxx, Mr. Cochrane and Mr. Perkins.

Hagen played the first nine holes more or less by instinct—and

on the ninth green found himself needing a short putt for a 30.
Looking up at the gallery, he noted with surprise and pleasure the
presence of three old friends, Jimmy Foxx, Mickey Cochrane and
Cy Perkins. The Haig beamed, and walked over to shake hands.
"Hiya, Jimmy. Hiya, Mike. Hiya, Cy," he yelled. "Haven't seen
you in a hell of a long time."

The three Athletics were convulsed by this second ceremony.
Their laughter faded into awe when they heard Hagen's score. He
sank the putt, took a 64 for the day, and won the tournament with
280. It was to be Hagen's last win in any big tournament.

But once in a while, in the few golfing years that were left to
him, the magic of his bold, sudden-death touch came back again.
Hagen was in his forties when he broke the course record at
Inverness, Scotland, with a 64. In 1943, at the age of 50, he
captained a pickup team against the American Ryder Cup team,
and shot a 71 in his first match. Thus, his career overlapped to a
degree those of the stars of the next generation. He saw them
all—and, with the cheerful arrogance of a giant of the days when
men were men, he gave them nothing. If they were brought
together in their respective primes, he says, he, Jones and Sarazen
could beat Snead, Hogan and Middlecoff, match or medal, for
money, chalk or marbles. Modern equipment and golf-course
engineering have lowered scores. But the fewer, cruder clubs of
the old days increased the skill of the players. And by playing in all
weathers, dirty and clean, they acquired a strength and wisdom,
down to the marrows of their bones, that the new men cannot
equal.

Until he settled in the house he lives in today—on Long Lake,
near Traverse City, Michigan, with big fish to the right of him and
tall highballs to the left and a sleek paunch like a Mongol
chieftain's—the Haig never had a permanent home. The need of
crowds, new crowds, with new faces and tastes (and new money),
kept him tramping about the world for years, to England, Ireland,
France, Scotland, Germany, Africa, Hawaii, Australia, New Zea-
land, China, the Philippines, Japan.

Even when he wasn't playing, the crowds still came to him. Johnny Farrell, himself a U.S. Open champion of the 1920's, was playing a major tournament one day, and burning up the course. Al Watrous walked over from a nearby tee to pass the time of day. "How's it going, Johnny?" he asked. "Terrific!" Farrell said. "I can't miss. Looks like I may break the course record."

"That's fine," Watrous said. He looked around. "Where's the crowd?" Farrell smiled philosophically. "Over behind the caddie house," he said, "watching Hagen play mumblety-peg."

The new men cannot hope to equal Hagen as a showman—but they play for big money today chiefly because Hagen boosted the price scale, by his showmanship. The Haig used to say: "Make the hard ones look easy, and the easy ones look hard." He did, and for 30 years, hard and easy, he made them all.

# A Room at the Barn
## *John McNulty*

James Thurber once wrote about John McNulty, "Cold type
could never do justice to such a man. When he told a tale of
people or places, it had a color and vitality that faded in the
retelling by anyone else." One of John's favorite places was
Belmont Park. Here we have him paying a visit to Belmont to
spend some time with a great race horse, Native Dancer, for
whom, as he says, "I have a deep fondness." When you get John
McNulty describing such an experience, you are bound to get a
memorable piece of writing. Only John would notice the groom
who pauses in his work to admire Native Dancer and then says
reassuringly to another thoroughbred in the Vanderbilt stable,
"You a good horse, too."

Once in a great while, a man all of a sudden finds himself completely happy and content. His stomach feels good; he's breathing
fine and easy; there's nothing whatever bothering him in his mind;
the sun is shining, perhaps, but it doesn't have to be; a breeze is
blowing gently, perhaps, but it doesn't need to be; and nearby
there is something or somebody he has a deep fondness for. What
he's fond of can be a boat, or a woman, or a horse—anything at all.
About eleven o'clock in the morning on Tuesday, April 14th, I was
silently grateful to find myself in that pleasant fix. At that hour, I
was sitting alone in a warm and comfortable room no more than
thirty yards away from the stall in which stood the race horse
Native Dancer. I have a deep fondness for Native Dancer.

Because of my feeling about the horse, I had long wanted to
know him better—pay him a visit and stay with him for a day or so.
That's not an altogether easy thing to do; my idea, in its way, was
like having the notion that it would be nice to drop in at the White

House for a weekend to see how things go around there. Nevertheless, through the intercession of friends, I had got permission to go and stay awhile with Native Dancer, who was then stabled at Alfred Gwynne Vanderbilt's barn at Belmont Park.

That Tuesday morning, I left my house in Manhattan about seven o'clock and, in a car driven by a friend, went out to the track, at Elmont, Long Island. It was a gray, chill morning, brightening slowly, with a fairly sharp wind nosing about. The gates at Belmont are closely guarded at all hours, and we were stopped there by uniformed attendants, who examined our credentials and then waved us inside, to the stable area of the vast racing plant.

A sign on the road that wound between dozens of long barns said:

SLOW

PLEASE CONSIDER

THE HORSES

So we went slowly, and here and there, as a group or "set" of horses hove into view on the way to or from the early-morning exercise at the track, we stopped until they passed. My friend pulled up at Barn 20, where two men were standing near two automobiles and chatting. The license number of one car was AG–2; the other's was ND 46–46. "That AG one is Mr. Vanderbilt's, for Alfred Gwynne Vanderbilt," said my companion, who is well versed in such matters. "The one with ND on it belongs to Bill Winfrey, Mr. Vanderbilt's trainer, and the ND, of course, is for Native Dancer, That's them, talking." In a few minutes, I was introduced to Mr. Vanderbilt and Mr. Winfrey. When I said, "Pleased to meet you, Mr. Winfrey," he corrected me. "I'm Bill Winfrey," he said. "Mr. Winfrey is a trainer over at Jamaica. He's my father."

"Make yourself at home," Mr. Vanderbilt said to me, cordially. "I got to be going along."

There is a well-made two-story brick dormitory a few yards from Barn 20, for the use of trainers, stable foremen, and some of the help. It contains two offices, and twenty-two rooms and four baths; half of it is occupied by the Vanderbilt people, and half by the Woodvale Farm people, whose barn is nearby. Bill Winfrey took me to a ground floor room he had been using and told me that it would be mine during my visit. He and his wife live in an apartment building about ten minutes away from the track.

That morning the sport pages had announced that if conditions were right, Native Dancer would run a public trial between the fifth and sixth races at the Jamaica track, which is currently holding its spring meeting. (Racing doesn't start at Belmont until May 6th.) Native Dancer had been scheduled to run in the fifth race at Jamaica the previous day, but only two owners had expressed a willingness to put their horses up against him, and the race had been cancelled. Mr. Vanderbilt requested that a public trial be substituted, and the Jamaica authorities had agreed, in order to satisfy the thousands of racegoers who wanted a look at Native Dancer. In the trial, Native Dancer was to take the track with two stablemates from Barn 20, break from the starting gate, as in a regular race, and run six furlongs, or three-quarters of a mile. It would be a make-believe race, with no betting, but—or so it was hoped—it would give Native Dancer the feeling of having been in a real race, and this was desirable, because, as Bill Winfrey explained as I unpacked, the horse had not raced since October 22nd. "He needs racing to tighten him up for what's ahead of him," Winfrey said.

Bill told me he was going to drive over to Jamaica, to see what the track was like, and that I could go along if I liked. "It's been raining a lot," he said as we got into ND 46–46, "and the track's still pretty wet. We'll go walk on it—see exactly how it feels." Driving along, he explained that he'd like to run the horse with his forelegs bandaged, and, for that reason, he didn't want a wet track. "It isn't that anything's the matter with the forelegs," he went on. "But sometimes a horse will rap himself running fairly fast. That is, he will clip the back of a foreleg with one of his hind hoofs and make a cut. Bandages on the forelegs tend to prevent that from happening. But if the track is wet, bandages naturally get wet, and tend to shrink up, and they're apt to squeeze too tight on the tendons, harmfully. Well, we'll look at the track and see."

At Jamaica, we stopped alongside the track at a point opposite the clubhouse, and clambered between the rails onto the track. Bill took eight or ten analytical steps on the sandy, loamy, and still wet surface. The wind was now blowing hard. "Oh, this is O.K.," he said happily. "This wind will do the trick more than sunshine. They'll harrow this up after every race, and the wind will get at it. Then the horses in the early races will toss it up, and the wind will get at it some more. So by the time we go on, it'll be all right. So far, O.K.; we'll go ahead and run him."

We climbed back through the rails and drove around the track to the offices, so Bill could notify the officials that he was willing to proceed with the public trial. As we walked through the office corridors, I noticed that horsemen who were gathered there greeted Bill with a cordiality tinged with friendly envy, which I attributed, no doubt correctly, to his being the trainer in whose hands fate had placed Native Dancer. An odd thing, though, was that they never mentioned that name. "How's the big horse?" some would ask, and others, "How's your gray horse doing?" To all of them, Bill answered, "First rate, so far." Last year, 1952, as a two-year-old, Native Dancer ran in nine races and won them all.

On the way back to Belmont, I asked Bill to tell me a little about himself—where he was born, and all that. He said he was born in Detroit in 1916, but his family had moved here soon after that, and he had gone to grammar school in Queens, at P.S. 108. "It's right across from Aqueduct," he said. "You can see its roof from the stands there. Later, for three or four months, I went to high school at John Adams, down the boulevard from Aqueduct. Then, my father being a horseman and all, we went down to Florida where there was a big fuss about letting me into high school without transfer papers from up in New York, and we didn't have the papers with us. Anyway, that gave me a chance to convince my folks that I wanted the race track more than high school, and they let me do it. I went to helping my father. Walking hots, and things like that." The phrase "walking hots" denotes one of the lowly and yet one of the necessary jobs at a race track. It means slowly walking a horse around and around, leading him by a shank, for an hour or more, until he cools off from a race or a workout.

When Bill was a little over sixteen, he got a license as a jockey; sixteen is as young as a jockey can be, by law. But his jockeyship was short-lived, Bill said. "When I got my license in Florida, in January, I weighed ninety-one pounds, and by Saratoga, in August, I was a hundred and ten. I was long on weight and short on ability—that's what it amounted to. I just plain wasn't any good as a jockey, but I turned out to be pretty good as an exercise boy, and I went along for a while at that." An exercise boy is a fellow, sometimes a former or future jockey but not always so, who rides race horses during their practice spins in the early mornings. I asked Bill what qualities he thought made a good exercise boy. He didn't answer right away. He has, I noticed soon after I met him, a mannerism that he indulges in whenever he's thinking something out, big or small. He holds his left hand up to his face, palm outward, and nibbles on the second joint of his little finger. He nibbled it now. "Well, at least ordinary skill at riding, but I think it's confidence that makes a good boy," he said finally. "A boy lacks confidence, he's apt to communicate that lack to the horse, I believe, which makes everybody nervous—horse, boy, trainer, everybody. A boy has confidence, he sits there feeling good, and the horse feels good because the boy's confidence imparts itself to the horse, and there you are. Confidence is probably the main thing. Bernie Everson, our boy for the gray horse, has it. Good boy. We trust him."

I said something then that has been said many times about the gray horse—that, conceivably, he might turn out to be one of the great race horses of all time. "He's got a lot yet to prove—got most of it yet to prove," Bill said, and after a pause, went on, still nibbling the knuckle of the little finger and driving with one hand. "Tell the truth, a man my age doesn't deserve a horse like him," he said. "I'm only thirty-seven, not quite that yet. My father, training horses all his life, is sixty-eight, and he never had the luck to handle a horse like him. And I know so many trainers—some seventy, seventy-five years old, training horses fifty years and more, working hard, knowing their business much more than I know it—who never had the luck to get one like this gray horse. Tell the truth, a man of thirty-seven doesn't deserve it, that's all. I've had good luck, and all I can do is hope it holds. Still, I don't want to get greedy for luck. I've had more than my share already. For instance, I came on with Mr. Vanderbilt at just the right time. I don't want to get technical with you, but for a long time Mr. Vanderbilt bred his horses according to one system, or method, or whatever you want to call it. Then he changed to another system. I wasn't with him when he changed; my luck was in the fact that I stepped into this job just when the fruits of the new system were ready to be harvested, and that's what's happening. Whether the gray horse would have done as well, or better, with some other trainer, I don't know. Nobody else knows, either."

I said that training a horse with such a record and such potentialities must give rise to a lot of worries. "I try to worry as little as I can," Bill said. "I think of it like this: Say we take every precaution we can think of against something happening to him; say we feed him as right as we know how; say we have the best men we can get to take care of him, the best to ride him in workouts, the best to ride him in his races—that way we give him every opportunity to do the great things. That's all we can do. From then on, it's out of our hands—turned over to luck, Providence, or whatever. That's all we can do, and we're trying to do it."

By then, we were back at Barn 20, and it was still only about ten o'clock in the morning. "Now let's go in and see him," Bill said.

Bill conducted me into the long barn and to Stall No. 6, where Native Dancer lives. We looked in at him standing cater-cornered across the boxlike stall, in deep straw. Kneeling beneath him, and adjusting the comfort-and-protection bandages he wears while resting was a large colored man, who glanced up at us and smiled a

greeting. "This is Lester Murray, who takes care of him," Bill said
to me, and Murray, while still going on with his work, kneeling
calmly beneath the horse's belly, acknowledged the introduction.
"I got some small chores to do," Bill said, "so I'll leave you here
with Murray."

I asked Murray how much Native Dancer weighs, and he told
me about eleven hundred and twenty-five pounds, or about ninety
pounds more than he weighed at the end of his two-year-old year.

"How high is he?" I asked. "How tall, I mean?"

"He'll go a little more than sixteen hands," Murray answered.
That means Native Dancer is a fairly big horse—five feet four or
more from the ground to the withers, which is that hump on a
horse's back just above the shoulders.

"Would you like to have a good look at him, sir?" Murray asked
me. "What did Mr. Winfrey say your name was, sir?"

"McNulty," I said.

"I mean your first name, sir."

"John."

"I'll turn him around, Mr. John, so you get a good look at him."

Murray got up and slapped the horse loudly on his massively
muscular rump. "Turn round, now, you big bum!" he said to him.
It was the rough tone of endearment some men use when they
greet a crony. Obediently, the horse swung around as far as he
could, considering that his halter was chained, loosely, to two
walls at one corner of the stall.

I believe that Native Dancer is handsome, majestic, fit to be
looked at for a long, long time, and looked at often, just for the
pleasure of seeing a living creature so marvellously contrived by
the millions of years that have passed since a horse was a creature
about eleven inches high. I thought he looked just wonderful,
though I have to confess that once race horses move off the pages of
the *Morning Telegraph* they are reasonably unfamiliar to me. He
is not a light gray, which is what most people think of when
someone mentions a gray horse. He is dark gray—almost black
here and there. Iron gray, some might say, but "iron" is too prosaic

a word. His face is quite light; sometimes, when seen from a certain angle, it appears to be a silvery mask. On his left side, just below and just behind where his saddle cloth sits during a race, there is a very light-gray design—something like a free-hand map of France. His tail is dark, with a shimmer of gray toward the end. There in the stall, he looked much bigger than he ever looks on the track. He was very calm as Murray knelt down again and went back to work on the bandages.

While Murray worked, he talked to the horse banteringly, in a kind of reassuring monotone with music in it. "Don't you lift up that old leg at me, you big old horse, you," he'd say. "Stand still there now, you big bum, stand still now, while I get this here bandage fixed up pretty and nice, stand still. You got work to do today, horse, and I'm gonna fix you up so you can do it right, like you always do."

A plump black cat strolled up beside me, stood there for a minute, and then, impudently, superciliously, stepped into the stall. Around her neck was a beautiful collar woven in two strands of leather, one cerise and one white, in a diamond pattern. Cerise and white are the Vanderbilt racing colors. Later, I learned that the harness maker for the stable outfits all the stable cats with these collars, which he fashions from old browbands once worn by the Vanderbilt racers as part of their full-dress regalia.

Murray finished his bandaging, stood up and stretched, and slapped a happy slap on the horse's rump. "Hello, you old cat!" he said, looking down at the cat. "Mr. John, let me tell you something. When we was coming back here all the way across the country, from Santa Anita, California, that old cat—we call her Mom—she come along with us. She had a little box in the car, not far from this horse. Once in a while, he'd lean over and nuzzle her in the back of her neck with his nose. That old cat's not afraid of him, and he don't mind her. Well, Mr. John, that Mom never in her life ever had anything but black kittens in her whole life. Then we get back here, and in a week that Mom have five kittens. And every single, solitary one of them gray! Gray like him! He's a powerful horse, he is."

Murray came out of the stall and said he was going to feed the gray horse about a half hour earlier than usual because of the doings that afternoon. Ordinarily, he explained, Native Dancer, along with the twenty-six other horses in the Vanderbilt barn, is fed at eleven in the morning, four in the afternoon, and one in the morning. This is a routine more or less peculiar to that particular stable. "Feeding him at one o'clock in the morning more or less lets him get his food digested up before his morning workout time," Murray said. "I'm going to cut him a little short on this feeding now. Usually he gets two quarts of oats at eleven o'clock, but this time I'll give him a quart and a half. Then, usually, he gets four quarts at four o'clock and four quarts more at one o'clock. That makes ten quarts altogether. Night watchman give him that one-o'clock stuff." He told me that the gray horse is a "good doer," which means that he has a fine appetite. He would eat more than ten quarts of oats a day if he could get it. Then, of course, there's his hay. The hayrack in his stall is filled twice a day, and he munches at it when he isn't resting—sort of a between-meals snack, the hay is. Later, Bill Winfrey told me that his hay consists of mixed clover until about four days before a race, when he is switched to plain timothy. "Timothy doesn't have any of those nice, sweet buds in it," Bill said. "With the clover hay, he's like a child with Tootsie Rolls, or something; he stuffs himself with it. The timothy is just straight food, and he's more sensible about that."

Murray got the quart and a half of oats ready, poured it into the feedbox, and then unfastened the halter chains so the horse could turn around and eat, which he did avidly. We both watched while he ground away the oats. Then Murray excused himself, to get some lunch, and Harry Walker, his second-in-command, took over. Walker, another big colored man, came in and took a look at the gray horse eating. "He doing good like always," he said.

Then Walker and I went into an office at the end of the line of stalls, and sat down in two chairs there, leaving the door open. "I set here and I can see every one of them stall doors," Walker said. "That's a rule—got to be somebody here every minute, keep an

eye on everything. Tom Drysdale, he the night watchman, he's
here all night." There was hardly a sound in that big barn, except
us talking and a few barn swallows or sparrows chirping and
making a soft flutter of wings as they swooped toward nests in the
eaves with bits of loot—wisps of hay, or some oats, or pieces of
string they got Lord knows where. There was a television set by
our side, but neither one of us thought of turning it on—not
interested. It was enough sitting there, looking down past the gray
horse, past all the others, smelling the clean, unforgettable smell
of grain and hay and liniment and ammonia and faint old aromatic
race-horse sweat. "I think I'll just walk down past all those horses
and look at them," I said to Walker. "Then I guess I'll go to my
room for a little rest."

"That's good," he said. "Just walk along and see 'em. Them
two-year-olds, they'll want to know who you are. But them others,
they won't care." I walked along past the stalls, and peeked in at
First Glance and Young Buck and Whence and Whither and Half
Caste and Lap of Luxury and the others. The two-year-olds turned
around and stared and the others didn't care. I went back to my
room for a while.

Back in the room, that was when the time came that I felt so
good that Tuesday morning. Very quiet it was in the room, just as
in the barn. I thought how Native Dancer looked, over in his stall,
thirty yards away or so. He was tuned so exquisitely he almost
thrummed standing still. I wonder how many people knew about
the gray horse. Millions, certainly, have heard of him, this
season's big three-year-old undefeated champ, and thousands,
like me, read all they could read about him and his coming quest
for the Triple Crown in the Derby, the Preakness, and the Belmont Stakes. They know that his sire was Polynesian and his dam
Geisha; that's where he gets the gray, from Geisha. They know
about the nine races he ran last year as an undefeated two-year-
old, and a few of them know to the dot his share of those purses,
which was $230,495. Thinking about that figure led me to specu-
late on how much the gray horse is worth, which, in turn, led me to

the conclusion that such speculation is foolish, because there were so many things about him that had no price. So I gave up this train of thought and went back and sat down with Harry Walker again.

It was getting to be time to take the gray horse and the others over to Jamaica for the public trial. Pretty soon, Bill Winfrey came along and outlined his plans for the run. He said that the two horses he would race against the big horse were Beachcomber and First Glance. Beachcomber is a three-year-old gelding who had never raced. "Sometimes he runs pretty fast for a short distance in the morning, though," Bill said. First Glance is a well-known handicap horse who has won some big races. He is cleverly named, being by Discovery out of Bride Elect. "The plan is this," Bill said. "We'll start from the gate, of course. The regular rider, Eric Guerin, will ride the gray horse. Bernie Everson will ride First Glance, and Albert Bao—that's one of our exercise boys —will ride Beachcomber. What I figure to do is to have Beachcomber get away from the gate fast and grab a lead on the gray horse and the other. Beachcomber won't go fast very far, and when the gray horse catches him, I'd like to have First Glance kind of take over and give the gray horse a run. That way, there'll be some sort of competition for the gray horse all through this thing. That is, if everything works out as planned, which it may not."

The van that was to take the horses to Jamaica hadn't come yet, so we strolled down to Stall No. 6. As we looked in, Murray was turning a bucket upside down and climbing onto it, on the off side of the gray horse. Standing on the bucket, and talking to the horse, Murray began to braid his mane. "Now I'm going to fix you up pretty, you big bum, before all those people look at you," he was saying. He worked away patiently, the horse hardly moving at all. Every once in a while, he'd wet his finger in his mouth and then moisten the braid. It took him about a half hour to fix the braid just right.

As Murray finished, the van pulled up outside the barn door. Big yellow van. A ramp was put against the side door of the van, and a heavy mat was laid down on the ramp. Wooden side railings, more than waist high on a man, were affixed to the ramp. John C. Mergler, the stable foreman, supervised operations, and Winfrey also stood by. Altogether, eight men took places in or near the van, as if they were taking battle stations. A horse could get hurt at a time like this. Native Dancer was the first to go into the van. He went up the ramp willingly, and as he went, Murray slapped him goodbye on the rump. The other two horses also went in easily, and the van door was closed and locked. The driver invited me to climb up in front with him, and we started off, taking Native Dancer to the races. Oh, well, to a make-believe race, anyway.

The other two horses didn't quite do their jobs in the public trial run. But after it was over, Bill Winfrey said it was all right, and that things hadn't worked out badly at all. When Fred. L. Capossela, the race announcer at Jamaica, said over the loudspeaker that Native Dancer was coming onto the track, horseplayers ran to the trackside from the mutuel windows where they had been engaged in the engrossing business of betting on the sixth race. Running out to see Native Dancer close to, they looked like hundreds of water bugs skating on the surface of a brook. The gray horse and the two others walked up the track and then around to the three-quarter pole, where the starting gate was standing. On a track, the three-quarter pole is a pole on the rail three-quarters of a mile from the finish line—not from the start, as a non-racegoing person might, and often does, think.

What happened was that when the three horses got off, Native Dancer jumped out of the gate ahead of the two others. Beachcomber never did catch up with him. Jockey Guerin had to hold the gray horse back tightly in order to let First Glance catch up. In that order—Native Dancer on the outside, First Glance on the inside and a little behind, and Beachcomber straggling in the rear—they went past the crowd and past the finish wire.

After we got back to Barn 20 in Belmont Park without a mishap, Bill and Murray and Walker and Mergler all felt the legs of the gray horse and found them O. K. The other men drifted away then, leaving Murray and me standing by Stall No. 6. "He keyed up," Murray said. "He a little mixed up in his mind, but he all right,

Mr. John. He don't know was that a race he was in, or wasn't it a race. They had the gate, they had them other two horses, and I guess they had the crowd yelling. Just the same, he don't know. He like a race, but he mixed up about *was* it a race."

Unconsciously, as he talked, Murray was cleaning a fleck of dirt off a bridle strap hanging by the stall door. I was looking down at his overalls. On his left pants leg, between the knee and the ankle, was fastened a row of shiny safety pins. They looked like some odd military decoration. They were, in reality, the badge of the man "who rubs horses." With the safety pins thus arranged, Murray, kneeling on his right knee beneath a horse, can reach for one handily to fasten a leg bandage. "You know what I think is missing in his mind, what got him mixed up in his mind, Mr. John?" he asked.

"No," I said.

"It all look like a race to him except one thing," Murray said. "They never brought him back to no winner's circle. Mr. John, this horse never been no place else but in that winner's circle. Every single, solitary time he run a race. He don't know what to make of it, no winner's circle this time. It got him mixed up in his mind."

When I awoke in my room at the stable the next morning, it was not yet fully daybreak. I turned on the bed light to look at my watch, and saw it was ten minutes to five. When I went to the window to close it against the morning chill, I heard three voices.

"Get an extry ring!" one voice said loudly as if to someone a long distance away.

"What kind of ring for what?" another voice said, far away.

"Extry coffee ring!" the first voice said.

"Oh, coffee bun?" the faraway one hollered back.

"Yuh, yuh, coffee bun—get an extry one!" the first voice said.

Then there was a third voice, this one singing. Five o'clock in the morning, the sun coming up, and the voice singing a blues—"Got nobody to call my own!"

After breakfast, I walked over toward the training track, which is adjacent to the Vanderbilt barn. A couple of stable hands were there beside the rail. On the far side of the track, in the gray morning, two horses were moving. In the grayness and the chill, one of the far-off horses was gray, too. Nobody mentioned his name. As the two horses came around the bend and into the stretch, the gray horse became grayer to the eye. The sound of hoofs hit sweetly on the ears. Although it is made by four hoofs, the gallop has a triple beat—"Tump-a-tum! Tump-a-tum! Tump-a-tum!" I watched and listened for a moment and then returned to the stable area.

Even before the big horse came back to the barn after the workout, his imminent approach was felt. It was in the air. "He coming back," I heard Murray say. Some of the men around the barn gathered outside to see if "he" was in sight yet. He was. He came down the road, between the barns, back to his home.

As Native Dancer passed each stall where a Vanderbilt horse was being groomed, work stopped for a few moments. "There he go," one groom said, pausing to watch, holding his currycomb in his right hand. Then he went back to work on his horse, and it was nice to hear him say, "You a good horse, too."

# Team Bobbing

## Edward J. Neil

The reporter who covers sports for the Associated Press wire
service does not often have the time or the freedom to compose
colorful literature. He must stick to the straight facts and get
them out fast with as few descriptive adjectives as possible.
Working within such tight limitations, Edward J. Neil, the great
AP sportswriter who was killed while covering the Spanish Civil
War, could still pack a brief dispatch with stirring suspense and
excitement. Here is his thrilling report on a ride in a bobsled
down a mountainside at seventy miles per hour during the 1932
Winter Olympic Games.

*Lake Placid, N.Y., February 2, 1932*
They took me down the most dangerous mile and a half in the
entire sports world today, gave me thrills enough to last a lifetime
and then before my eyes laid the picture of destruction that might
well have come to me from less capable hands.

It was 7 o'clock in the morning, deadly cold on the top of Mount
Van Hoevenberg, and the bobsledders of eight nations, men who
can't have nerves, laughed and chatted in a polyglot of French,
German, Swiss, Rumanian, Belgian, Italian, Austrian and English.

At their feet lay the Frankenstein contraptions known as bobsleds, 500 pounds of steel and oak. In the air was a fine mist of
snow. We were at the start of the Olympic bob slide, the mile and a
half of glare ice twisting through twenty-five awesome bends and
hairpin curves down the mountainside, the racing strip that in two
days has sent eight Germans to the hospital.

They watch the starter with his red flag and suddenly he gets word from a telephone strung along the slide that all is clear.

"Get ready," he yells. "To the mark. Harry Homberger's Red Devils."

Harry—they call him Hank—winks.

"You ask for it. Let's go."

He's just a pleasant kid, twenty-six years old, but a civil engineer from Saranac Lake, the fellow who built this slide. He is a pilot, four lives and a steering wheel in his grasp.

They say he's the greatest bobsled driver in the history of the sport—dark, keen-eyed, quiet. He is the Albie Booth of bobsleds, 168 pounds, but his shoulders are the widest in the crew. His world record is 1.52 for one and a half miles.

Hank climbs behind the wheel, we settle on the sled, bracing feet, gripping the straps on the side with hands shielded in padded gloves. I was No. 3, sandwiched in between huge Percy Bryant and the brakeman, Ed Horton, who yanks the steel jaws that clutch at the ice when we need to slow down.

Solemnly the men of other nations who can't hope to equal Homberger's skill shake our hands. They do that before each run; they act as though they never expected to see you again.

Particularly does Fritz Grau, German captain, make it a point to slap our backs. So did Albert Brehme, Hellmuth Hoppmann, the jovial Rudolph Krotki, the German team masseur who takes Max Ludwig's place for the day. An hour later they were all in a hospital.

Hank turns for a last word. "It's not so fast today," he says, "but I'll do my best to give you a thrill."

One heave and we're off. The foreigners clash for places around the telephone. Each station calls off our progress. I've watched them stand there tense, silent, seeming to be praying there'll be no shout: "They jumped a bank!" That means you've smashed through a curve going a mile a minute and your body is hurtling down a mountainside studded with rocks and trees and ice. I saw that, too, later.

Swiftly we pick up speed on the first straight drop. We're

shooting down what looks like a culvert of solid ice with the top half
cut off. The steel runners begin to sing. The wind tears at your
hunched head. Forty, fifty, sixty miles an hour.

"Lean," screamed Horton in my ear.

Up into my face came a dazzling wall of white ice. I leaned
hard. We sweep up to the top. The runners slide, catch. We hurtle
down again. That was the turn called Eyrie.

Now it's sixty again and going up, and one after another come
the blinding banks, ten, twenty, thirty feet high. Desperately I
leaned. This way, that way, gasping for breath, helpless, straining.
The wind is blinding. Tears stream from your eyes. You think you
can't hold on another second. You fight, surge, and then you're out
of the curve and flying down a straightaway, seventy miles an
hour, and you get a breath.

Then something begins to happen to your nervous system. The
curves are getting steeper. You're taking them eagerly. Suddenly
you begin to tingle; every nerve in your body feels as though some
one were playing on it with the bow of a fiddle. Exultation sweeps
up from your toes, reaches your throat. Back goes your head and
you howl with the sheer joy of it.

You're ready now for the serious part. "Whiteface," a vertical
semicircle of ice thirty-five feet high at seventy miles an hour. The
sky suddenly turned to a sheet of ice over your head, the track a
streak of blue under one elbow.

"Shady Corner," again at seventy, a thud as you fly into the wall,
smash off again, and just when you think you're gone, another
straightaway, another breath.

Then the final test, a final surge of every drop of blood through
your veins, the apex of sporting thrills and the end of many a
bobsled career—"Zigzag"—a whip to the left, a leap of five feet, all
four runners off the ground, to straighten out, a whip to the right,
one last burst and you're at the finish—limp, exhausted.

"Slow," said Hank, "about two minutes."

"Yes," said Horton, "I wish I'd brought my gun. I saw a rabbit I
could have got when we were going through Shady."

We started back up the mountain. Almost to Shady we heard

another bob screaming down the course. We jumped behind the
track peering through the snow up the twisted ice ribbon. We
could see Shady up the bend.

A bob flew into the turn at seventy miles an hour, swerved,
runners shrieked. The sled swept up the incline, smashed through
the top, four bodies hurled through the air, into a deep ravine
below. It was our friends, the Germans, Grau, Brehme, Hoppmann and Krotki.

We raced up the slide, helped carry the battered, blood-soaked
unconscious forms to the ambulances.

"That's the way it goes," Homberger sighed. Twenty minutes
later they're racing down again.

# My Favorite Caddie

## Gene Sarazen with
## Herbert Warren Wind

Here is Gene Sarazen's story of how an elderly English caddie named Skip Daniels guided him to one of the greatest triumphs of his golfing career, his 13-under-par, record-breaking victory in the 1932 British Open. A moving account of a close personal relationship between a champion golfer and a champion caddie, this is also a remarkable piece of writing about championship golf. The winner was Gene Sarazen, but the writing was done by Herbert Warren Wind, who invariably hits the ball straight down the middle of the fairway when he reports on golf for *The New Yorker*.

My story of the 1932 British Open actually begins in 1928 when I made a crossing to Europe with Walter Hagen. One evening during our voyage we were having a drink in the smoking room of the *Berengaria*, waiting for the auction pool to begin, when our conversation turned to the approaching British Open. "That is one title I want on my books, Walter," I confided to the man who had won that championship in 1922 and 1924. "I've invested thousands of dollars coming over for it, and I'll probably go right on doing it until I win that title or get too old to play. If there's any one thing I want to accomplish in golf, it's to win the British Open."

Walter smiled at my earnestness. "Gene, you can never win the British Open," he said, "unless you have a caddie like the ones I've had." He tested the new pinch of Scotch that the waiter had set before him. "Now, Gene, I'll tell you what I'll do. I've won the

British Open a couple of times, so winning it again doesn't mean as much to me as it does to you. I'll loan you my caddie, Skip Daniels. He's an old fellow, caddies only in the county of Kent, just at Sandwich, Deal, and Prince's, no other courses. He's very particular about the men he caddies for. It's got to be someone special, like the Prince of Wales or Walter Hagen. Skip expects to caddie for me at Sandwich this year, but I think I can arrange it with him to caddie for you instead. One thing more. He's a very expensive caddie. He'll cost you at least thirty or forty pounds."

Hagen went into a few details on Daniels' personality and on his infallible judgment in the 1922 Open. I felt great. I knew how important a caddie can be in winning any championship, especially on a foreign course.

I arrived at Sandwich early and asked the caddiemaster for Daniels. "I'm afraid you can't have Skip," the caddiemaster replied. "He's Walter Hagen's caddie." I told him that Hagen had agreed to loan me Skip for the Open, but no assignment was made until the caddiemaster had checked with Hagen personally. Then he introduced me to Daniels near the pro shop. Daniels tipped his hat. If he felt heartbroken at learning that he wouldn't be working with Hagen, he didn't show it.

He was an old boy, all right, around sixty or sixty-one, old even for a professional British caddie. He wore a weather-beaten cap, an old celluloid collar, and a black oxford suit that had never been pressed in its lifetime. I think I fell in love with him at first sight.

Daniels had a wonderful effect on me during the ten days of practice that we put in before the start of the Open. He had an enthusiasm I had rarely seen in caddies a third of his age. He limped slightly, but after I had hit out a batch of balls, he would trot down the practice field to retrieve them and then trot back to the tee. He knew instinctively how to inspire his man with confidence. "I've never seen Hagen hit the shots as well as you're hitting them, sir," he would say after an afternoon's workout. He did much more than carry his player's bag. He could tell you what you were doing wrong with a shot, and he'd tell it to you in a very nice way. In the evenings after dinner we would stroll out on the course with a putter and a dozen balls and practice on various greens. Daniels would point out places where he'd done patrol duty, guarding against a possible enemy invasion, during World War I. He knew every blade of grass along that stretch of Kentish coast. He had lived in the bunkers and knew them as he knew his own home.

Daniels and I had become very close friends by the eve of the championship. I made up my mind that I would follow his advice at all times. I knew that if I did I couldn't go wrong. He kept buoying my confidence with his own genuine confidence in my ability to win. I remember his final pep talk: "I've watched Walter practicing, sir. He's recovering very well, but he's not hitting the ball like you are. We should have no trouble beating him, and he's the man to beat."

Daniels and I played a heady first round of 72. We were moving at the same sanguine pace on the second day when I pulled my drive on the fourteenth into the rough. This fourteenth hole, a par 5, is called Suez Canal because of the deep ditch that traverses the fairway some seventy yards or so before the green. I looked over my lie in the rough, took in the distance to the Canal, and concluded that I could carry it if I cracked a good wood out of the rough. Daniels shook his head. "But, Dan, if I can get a birdie here," I said to him, "I can beat Jurado and lead the field." Daniels shook his head again, and tapped the blade of the mashie, or 5 iron, in my bag. "This is no time to lead the field," he said. "Tomorrow night is when you want to be in front, sir." I said stubbornly, "No, Dan, I'm going for it." I yanked my spoon out of the bag. I dug my spikes in and swatted the ball hard with my spoon. The tall, thick rough snuffed the ball before it could get started, and it squished only 20 yards, still in the rough. I lashed out quickly with my spoon again, giving Daniels no chance to cool me off. I got the ball out of the rough this time, but that was about all. I finally ended up with a 7 on the hole. I could see from Dan's eyes that he was heartbroken. I had disregarded his advice to play a mashie shot from the rough safely short of the Canal, and follow it with an easy pitch to the green that would have left me with a putt for a 4, or a sure 5. Dan tried to cheer me up as we started down the fifteenth fairway. "We can make that up, Mr. Sarazen," he said. I knew he was really saying to himself, "That's why Hagen beats this fellow."

Dan settled me down and I finished the round in 76. He coached me to a 73 on the third round the next day, putting me only one stroke behind the leader, Hagen. I felt confident during the luncheon interval between the third and the fourth, or final, round that I was playing well enough to overtake Hagen. In my room at the Guilford Hotel I went over an acceptance speech with John Ford, the motion picture director, because the Prince of Wales was to present the cup to the winner, and I didn't know the proper etiquette for responding.

Hagen started his final round about an hour and a half before I teed off. I made the turn in 36, and as I was walking down the twelfth fairway, I saw a sleek limousine drive up with the Prince of Wales in the back seat. With the Prince was Hagen, wrapped up in his polo coat, which had huge mother-of-pearl buttons. They had come out to watch me finish. According to Daniels, I was Hagen's last serious challenger. Walter had visited at least seven traps on his last round and had still scored a 72. I stayed with par figures until I reached the 69th hole, but there I slipped to a stroke over par, and Walter had his Third British Open safely tucked away.

The difference between our total final scores, 292 and 294, was due to my boneheaded refusal to heed Daniels' advice on the Suez Canal. I admitted this to Dan as we said goodbye after the presentation ceremony. There were tears in Dan's eyes when he said to me, "We'll try it again, sir, won't we? Before I die, I'm going to win an Open championship for you."

In 1932 the British Open was scheduled to be held on the links of the Prince's Club in Sandwich, right next door to the Royal St. George course where I had lost and Hagen had won in 1928.

Daniels would be available at Prince's if I decided to take another crack at the British Open, but I wasn't so certain that I cared to knock my brains out any more trying to win that ornery championship. I had failed in the Open at Muirfield in 1929, and, in 1931 at Carnoustie, where I had played pretty fair golf, I again trailed the winner, Tommy Armour, by two strokes. There were other considerations. Money was scarce in 1932 and getting scarcer, and I was in no mood to squander away the bank account that I had been able to build up slowly with my labors on the winter circuit.

It was Mary, my wife, who decided that I should go again to the British Open. Mary sat me down in our living room and assumed her best I-am-talking-business-so-be-prepared-to-take-me-seriously voice. "Gene, I don't believe I've ever seen you playing better than you are right now," she said, starting off on a very good foot. "I know how hard you've been working on keeping in condition, running up and down the front hall stairs, swinging that heavy club morning, noon and night, cutting yourself down to one cigar a day. Now don't interrupt me, Gene. Last week I was talking with Tom and Frances Meighan and they agree with me that your golf is better than it ever was and that you ought to play in the British Open."

"That's all very well and good," I said, "but what about the financial side of such a trip? This isn't any time to throw away a couple of thousand dollars, Mary. It would cost me just about that to cover all my expenses. I don't see it."

"I've given that a lot of thought, too," Mary said. "I decided it would be a good investment, everything considered." She stopped for a moment, and felt me out with a smile. "Now, Gene, I've got your tickets and your hotel reservations all taken care of. The only thing you have to do is get your passport fixed up. You're sailing a week from tomorrow on the *Bremen*."

I had a smooth crossing, and an enjoyable one, thanks to the lively company of Fred Astaire. In London, the first man I ran into at the Savoy was Roxy, a crony from Lakeville and a fanatic golf fan.

Roxy was going to play at Stoke Poges the next day and persuaded me to come along.

When we arrived at Stoke Poges, a young caddie—he was about twenty-seven, a stripling among British caddies—grabbed my bag. We whistled around the course in 67. "I'm going to caddie for you in the Open," the young man informed me when the round was over. "I know just the type of caddie you need, Mr. Sarazen."

My mind flashed back to Daniels. "You're a very smart caddie," I told the aggressive young man. "But I've already got a caddie for the Open. Skip Daniels."

"Oh, I know Daniels. He must be around sixty-five now."

"Just about," I said.

"He's too old to carry this bag," the young caddie said. "His eyesight is gone. On top of that, I heard he's been ill. Why don't you let me caddie for you at Prince's? I don't want to run Daniels down, but he'd ruin your chances if you took him on. The way you played today, you can't miss."

He had something there. That 67 had been as solid a round as I had ever played in England. If I could keep that up, no one would touch me in the Open.

I told the young man to meet me at Prince's.

After a few days in London, I went down to Prince's to practice. The first person I met there, right at the gate, was Daniels. He was overjoyed to see me. While we were exchanging news about each other, I could see that the last four years had taken a severe toll of him. He had become a very old man. His speech was slower. That shaggy mustache of his was much grayer. His limp was much more obvious. And his eyes didn't look good.

"Where's your bag, sir?" Daniels asked, hopping as spryly as he could toward the back seat of my auto.

"Dan," I said—I couldn't put it off any longer though I almost didn't have the heart to say it—"Dan, this bag is too heavy for you. I know you've been in bad health, and I wouldn't want you to try and go seventy-two holes with it."

Dan straightened up. "Righto, sir, if you feel that way about it," he said. There was great dignity in the way he spoke but you couldn't miss the emotion in his voice.

"I'm sorry, Dan," I said, and walked away. I had dreaded the thought of having to turn old Dan down, but I had never imagined that the scene would leave me reproaching myself as the biggest heel in the world. I attempted to justify what I had done by reminding myself that business was business and I couldn't afford to let personal feelings interfere with my determination to win the British Open. But that didn't help much.

I was a hot favorite to win. The American golf writers thought I had a much better chance than Armour, the defending champion, and Macdonald Smith, the other name entry from the States. George Trevor of the New York *Sun*, for example, expressed the belief that "Prince's course, a 7,000-yard colossus, will suit Sarazen to a tee, if you will pardon the pun. It flatters his strong points—powerful driving and long iron second shots." The English experts were also strong for me until, during the week of practice, they saw my game decline and fall apart. The young caddie from Stoke Poges did not suit me at all. I was training for this championship like a prizefighter, practicing in weather that drove the other contenders indoors, swinging the heavy club, doing roadwork in the morning. My nerves were taut and I was in no mood to be condescended to by my caddie. He would never talk a shot over with me. He just pulled a club out of the bag without a word, as if he were above making a mistake. When I would find myself 10 yards short of the green after playing the club he selected, he would counter my criticism that he had under-clubbed me by declaring dogmatically, "I don't think you hit that shot well." I began getting panicky as the tournament drew closer and my slump grew deeper. I stayed on the practice fairway until my hands hurt.

Something was also hurting inside. I saw Daniels in the galleries during that tune-up week. He had refused to caddie for any other golfer. He would switch his eyes away from mine when our glances met, and shuffle off to watch Mac Smith or another challenger. I continued to play with increasing looseness and petulance. The qualifying round was only two days off when Lord Innis-Kerr came to my hotel room on a surprise visit. "Sarazen, I have a message for you," Innis-Kerr said, with a certain nervous formality. "I was talking with Skip Daniels today. He's heartbroken, you know. It's clear to him, as it's clear to all your friends, that you're not getting along with your caddie. Daniels thinks he can straighten you out before the bell rings."

I told His Lordship that I had been thinking along the same lines. Daniels could very well be the solution.

"If it's all right with you, Sarazen," Lord Innis-Kerr said, "I'll call Sam, the caddiemaster, and instruct him to have Daniels meet you here at the hotel tomorrow morning. What time do you want him?"

"Have him here at seven o'clock," I said. "And thanks, very much."

Dan was on the steps of the hotel waiting for me the next morning. We shook hands and smiled at each other. "I am so glad we are together again," old Dan said. "I have been watching you since you arrived, and I know you've been having a difficult time with that boy." We walked to the course, a mile away. Sam, the caddiemaster, greeted me heartily and told me how pleased everybody was that I had taken Daniels back. "We were really worried about him, Mr. Sarazen," Sam said. "He's been mooning around for days. This morning he looks ten years younger."

Dan and I went to work. It was miraculous how my game responded to his handling. On our first round I began to hit the ball again. I broke par as Dan nursed me through our afternoon round. "My, but you've improved since 1928!" Dan told me. "You're much straighter, sir. You're always on line now. And I notice this afternoon that you're much more confident than you used to be recovering from bunkers. You have that shot conquered now." After dinner, I met Dan by the first tee and we went out for some putting practice.

The next day, the final day of preparation, we followed the same pattern of practice. I listened closely to Dan as he showed me how I should play certain holes. "You see this hole, sir?" he said when we came to the eighth. "It can be the most tragic hole on the course." I could see that. It was only 453 yards, short as par 5s go, but the fairway sloped downhill out by the 200 yard mark, and then, about 80 yards in front of the green, there was a massive chain of bunkers rising 25 to 35 feet high, straddling the fairway and hiding the green.

"But you won't have any trouble on this hole," Dan said. "You don't have to worry about the downhill lie when you make your second shot. You can use a shallow-face wood there. You can get the ball up quickly with that club. I should warn you, however, that those bunkers have been the graveyard of many great players. If we're playing against the wind, and we can't carry them, you must play safe. You cannot recover onto the green from those bunkers."

Yes, I thought as Dan spoke, the eighth could be another Suez.

That evening when the gathering darkness forced us off the greens and we strolled back to my hotel, Dan and I held a final pow-wow.

"We can win this championship, you and I," I said to Dan, "if we do just one thing."

"Oh, there's no doubt we can win it, sir," Dan said.

"I know, but there's one thing in particular that we must concentrate on. Do you remember that 7 at the Suez Canal?"

"Do I!" Dan said, putting his hand over his eyes. "Why, it's haunted me!"

"In this tournament," I said, "we've got to make sure that if we go over par on a hole, we go no more than one over par. If we can avoid taking another disastrous 7, Dan, I don't see how we can lose. You won't find me going against your advice this time. You'll be calling them and I'll be playing them."

Mac Smith and Tommy Armour were sitting on the front porch when we arrived at the hotel. "Hey, Skip," Armour shouted at the caddie. "How's Eugene playing?"

"Mr. Sarazen is right on the stick," Dan answered, "right on the stick."

The qualifying rounds were to be played one round on Royal St. George's and one round on Prince's. There isn't much to say about my play on that first day at Prince's. I had a 73, one under par. However, I shall never forget the morning of the second qualifying round. I looked out of my window at the Royal St. George's links as I was shaving and saw that the wind was shipping sand out of the bunkers and bending the flags. A terrific gale was blowing in from the North Sea. Then I saw a man in a black suit bent over against the wind, pushing his way from green to green. It was Daniels, diagramming the positions of the pins so that I would know how to play my approach shots. I qualified that day among the leaders. You have to play well when you are partnered with a champion.

That night the odds on my winning the Open, which had soared to 25–1 during my practice slump, dropped to 6–1, and Bernard Darwin had written in *The Times*, "I watched Sarazen play eight or nine holes and he was mightily impressive. To see him in the wind, and there was a good fresh wind blowing, is to realize how strong he is. He just tears the ball through the wind as if it did not exist."

On the day that the championship rounds began, the wind had died down to an agreeable breeze, and Daniels and I attacked from the very first hole. We were out in 35, one under par, with only one 5 on that first nine holes. We played home in 35 against a par of 38, birdieing the seventeenth and the eighteenth. My 70 put me a stroke in front of Percy Alliss, Mac Smith and Charlie Whitcombe. On the second day I tied the course record with a 69. I don't know how well Dan's old eyes could really see at a long distance, but he called the shots flawlessly by instinct and experience. I went one stroke over par on the ninth when I missed a curling 5-foot putt,

but that was the only hole on which we took a "buzzard." We made
the turn in 35 and then came sprinting home, par, par, birdie, par,
par, birdie, birdie, birdie, par. My halfway total, 139, gave me a
three shot margin over the nearest man, Alliss, four over Whitcombe, and five over Archie Compston, who had come back with a
70 after opening with a 74. Armour had played a 70 for a 145, but
Tommy's tee shots were giving him a lot of trouble—he had been
forced to switch from his driver to his brassie—so I did not figure
on too much trouble from him. Mac Smith had started his second
round with a 7 and ended up with a 76. That was too much ground
for even a golfer of Mac's skill and tenacity to make up.

The last day now, and the last two rounds. I teed off in the
morning at nine o'clock. Three orthodox pars. A grand drive on the
fourth, and then my first moment of anguish. I hit my approach on
the socket. Daniels did not give me a second to brood. "I don't
think we'll need that club again, sir," he said matter-of-factly. I
was forced to settle for a 5, one over par, but with Daniels holding
me down, I made my pars easily on the fifth and sixth and birdied
the seventh.

Now for the eighth, 453 yards of trouble. So far I had handled it
well, parring it on both my first and second rounds. Daniels had
given me the go-ahead to use my brassie on both my blind shots
over the ridge of bunkers, and each time I had carried that hazard.
On this third round, I cracked my drive down the middle of the
billowy fairway. Daniels handed me my spoon after he had looked
the shot over and tested the wind, and pointed out to me the
direction to the pin hidden behind the bunkers. I hit just the shot
we wanted, high over the ridge of bunkers and onto the green,
stopping about 30 feet from the cup. When I stroked the putt up to
the hole, it caught a corner and dropped for an eagle 3. My
momentum from that eagle carried me on to a birdie 3 on the
ninth. Out in 33. Okay. Now to stay there.

After a nice start home, I wobbled on the 411-yard thirteenth,
pulling my long iron shot to the left of the green and taking a 5. I
slipped over par again on the 335-yard fifteenth, three-putting

from 14 feet when I went too boldly on a putt for a birdie and missed the short one coming back. I atoned for these lapses by birdieing the sixteenth and the eighteenth to complete that long second nine in 37, one under par, and the round in 70, four under. With eighteen more holes left to go, the only man who had a chance to catch me was Arthur Havers, five strokes behind with 74–71–68. Mac Smith, fighting back with a 71, was in third place but 8 shots away. Alliss had taken a 78 and was out of the hunt.

If the pressure and the pace of the tournament was telling on Dan, he didn't show it. I found him at the first tee after lunch, raring to get back on the course and wrap up the championship. We got off to an auspicious start on that final round—par, birdie, par, par. On the fifth I went one over par, shook it off with a par on the sixth, but when I missed a 4 on the seventh, I began to worry about the possible errors that I might make. That is a sure sign that a golfer is tiring. That eighth hole with the bunkers was ahead of us again and I was wondering if it would catch up with me this time.

I drove well, my ball stopping a few feet short of the spot where I had played my second shot with the spoon in the morning round. Daniels took his time weighing the situation and then drew the spoon from the bag again. I rode into the ball compactly and breathed a sigh of relief as I saw it rise up quickly and clear the bunkers with yards to spare.

"That's how to play golf, sir," Daniels said, winking an eye approvingly. "That's the finest shot you've played on this hole."

He was right, of course. We found out, after climbing up and over the ridge of bunkers, that my ball was only 8 feet from the cup. I holed the putt for my second eagle in a row on that hole and then made a standard par on the ninth for a 35.

Only nine more now. One over on the tenth. Nothing to fret about. Par. Par. Par. A birdie on the fourteenth. One over on the fifteenth, three putts. One over on the sixteenth, a fluffed chip shot. On the seventeenth tee, Daniels slowed me down and spoke to me. "We're going to win this championship, sir. I have no worries on that score. But let's make our pars on these last two holes. You always play them well."

A par on the seventeenth. On the eighteenth a good drive into the wind, a brassie shot right onto the green, and down in two putts for a birdie and a round of 35–39–74, even par for the course. There was no challenge to my total of 283. Mac Smith, the runner-up, was five strokes higher and Havers was a stroke behind Mac.

Feeling like a million pounds and a million dollars, respectively, Daniels and I sat down on a bank near the first tee and congratulated each other on a job well done. Our score of 283 was 13 under par on a truly championship course, and it clipped two strokes off the previous British Open record, Bob Jones' 285 at St. Andrews in 1927. As much as I was thrilled by setting a new record, I was even more elated because I had led all the way and had encountered no really rocky passages because I had had the excellent sense to listen to Daniels at every puzzling juncture. Through his brilliant selection of clubs and his understanding of my temperament, I had been able to keep my resolution to go no more than one stroke over par on any hole. The eighth hole, which I had feared might be another Suez, had turned out to be my best friend. I had two 3s and two 5s there, a hole where I would have gladly settled for four 6s. And, as a matter of fact, there was not one 6 on my scorecard for the whole four rounds of the championship tournament.

When the officials told me that they were ready to begin the presentation ceremony on the porch of the clubhouse, I asked them if Daniels could stand beside me as I received the trophy. I explained that it had really been a team victory. The officials were sympathetic but they explained that having a caddie participate in the award ceremony would be against British tradition. I scanned the crowd gathering before the clubhouse, looking for Dan so that at least I could take him to a front row seat. I couldn't find him. Then, just as the tournament officials were beginning to get impatient about the delay that I was causing, I spotted Dan coming down the driveway on his bicycle, carrying a grandson on each handlebar. On with the show.

After the ceremony, the team of Daniels and Sarazen got together for a rather tearful goodbye. I gave Dan my polo coat, and told him that I would be looking for him the next year at St. Andrews. I waved to him as he pedaled happily down the driveway, the polo coat flapping in the breeze. There was a good-sized lump in my throat as I thought of how the old fellow had never flagged for a moment during the long grind of the tournament, and how, pushing himself all the way, he had made good his vow to win a championship for me before he died.

It was the last time I saw Dan. A few months later some English friends wrote to tell me that he had passed away after a short illness. They said that after the Open he had worn the polo coat continually, even when he was in a pub telling golf fans the story of how "Sarazen and I did it at Prince's." When old Dan died, the world was poorer by one champion.

# Stymie—
# Common Folks

## *Joe H. Palmer*

Here is the late New York *Herald Tribune*'s wonderful racing
writer, the late Joe Palmer, paying a tribute to a wonderful race
horse, Stymie, who won his handicaps the hard way. "Give him
a field with speed in it, at a mile and a half or more," Joe wrote,
"and horses had better get out of his way, even Whirlaway."
Plenty of people around the race tracks are still paying tributes
to Joe Palmer, lifting their glasses of Kentucky bourbon—even
the ones who usually prefer Scotch. "It keeps happening all the
time," a man at Belmont Park said recently. "Something comes
up around the track and I think, 'What a shame Joe isn't here to
write about that.' "

On the cold blustery afternoon of January 28, 1921, several hundred persons huddled in the wind-swept stands of the old Kentucky Association track at Lexington to see one horse gallop past
them. Down he came, a great red chestnut with a copper mane
and a high head, flying the black and yellow silks of Samuel D.
Riddle. This was Man o' War, leaving the race tracks forever.

Fourteen years passed before Lexington considered another
horse worth a turnout. Then, on March 11, 1935, some five
hundred citizens assembled, on a foul, wet afternoon, to see
Equipoise take his last public gallop. This was at the private track
of the C. V. Whitney farm, because it was in that unbelievable
two-year period when Lexington had no public race track.

The next performance, and as far as I know the last one, came on

August 8, 1943, when Calumet Farm celebrated "Whirlaway Day." By this time the Chamber of Commerce had got into the act, and there was a remarkable spate of Congressmen, Southern oratory, news cameras and radio announcers. This is not a complete list.

It is unlikely (though you can never tell about a Chamber of Commerce) that there will be any such doings over Stymie, when he arrives to enter the stud at Dr. Charles Hagyard's Green Ridge Farm. It isn't that the other three were Kentuckians coming home, and that Stymie's an outlander from Texas. It was thoroughly appropriate that Stymie should have his final public appearance at Jamaica, because he's a Jamaica kind of horse. Though I have no doubt he will do well in the stud, his kinship is with the race track, not the breeding farm.

Man o' War, Equipoise and Whirlaway all were equine royalty from the day they were foaled. Stymie was common folks. It is true that he carries the blood of both Equipoise and Man o' War, but all pedigrees are purple if you go back a little. He was the son of a horse that had won two common races, out of a mare that couldn't win any. Nobody ever thought the first three were anything but good. Stymie began as a fifteen hundred dollar plater that couldn't get out of his own way.

Stymie wasn't, of course, as good as any of the three. But he was immeasurably tougher. Could he have got to the races one more time, he would have started as many times as all three of the others together. If you want to clutter your mind with a perfectly useless bit of information, Man o' War made his reputation by blazing nineteen miles and five furlongs; Equipoise, stopping now and then to grow a new hoof, ran just a trifle over fifty miles in competition. Whirlaway lasted a little longer and lacked half a furlong of running sixty-six miles. But Stymie's journey to leadership among the world's money winners took him 142 miles, plus half a furlong and sixty yards. That's more than the other three together.

Man o' War and Equipoise and Whirlaway each won the first

time out, at short odds, as they were expected to do. Stymie was 31 to 1 in a $2,500 claiming race and he ran as he was expected to do, too, finishing seventh. He was out fourteen times before he could win, and that was a $3,300 claimer.

You are not to imagine that Stymie was accidentally and mistakenly dropped into a claiming race before any one appreciated his quality. He ran twelve times in claiming races and got beat in eleven of them. He was, until the fall of his two-year-old season, right where he belonged. Then, from this beginning, he went on to win $918,485.

This is, you will see, basically the story of the ugly duckling, of Cinderella among the ashes, of Dick Whittington and his cat, and of all the world's stories none has ever been preferred to that which leads to the public and very glorious triumph of the oppressed and the downtrodden. Jamaica's horseplayers are to some extent oppressed and downtrodden, and perhaps in Stymie they find a vicarious success.

The horse envisioned by a breeder, in Kentucky, or elsewhere, is the son of a Derby winner out of an Oaks mare, which can sweep the futurities at two and the classics at three, and then come back to the stud to send other great racers to the wars. These are, roughly, the specifications which fit such horses as Citation and Count Fleet and War Admiral, and the like.

But the race-trackers, I think, save most of their affection for the Exterminators and the Stymies and the Seabiscuits, who do it the hard way in the handicaps, pounding out mile after bitter mile, giving weight and taking their tracks wet or dry, running for any jockey, and trying with what they've got, even when they haven't got enough. That's why Stymie fitted a farewell at Jamaica better than a welcome in Kentucky.

He's a curious horse, this obscurely bred Texas product. This tourist leaned on Jack Skinner's back fence at Middleburg one December for maybe a half hour, just studying Stymie, who did not return the compliment, but went on picking at the scanty winter grass. Except for the crooked blaze which gives him a devil-may-care expression, he's the most average horse you ever saw. Not tall, not short, not long, not close-coupled. Good bone, good muscle, good chest—nothing outstanding, nothing poor. As a result, of course, he is almost perfectly balanced, and maybe this is what makes him tick.

However, there is another matter. When Stymie comes to the peak of condition, he exudes vitality so you expect to hear it crackle. He comes to a hard, lean fitness that you seldom see in domestic animals, unless in a hunting dog that has been working steadily, or perhaps a hunter that has been having his ten miles a day over the fields. This is when, as Hirsch Jacobs says, he gets "rough." It isn't temper or meanness. He just gets so full of himself that he wants things to happen.

The faster he goes the higher he carries his head, which is all wrong according to the book, but is a characteristic of the tribe of Man o' War, to which he is inbred. This tourist, who doesn't scare easily in print, will long remember the way Stymie came around the turn in the Pimlico Cup Handicap with his copper mane flying in the wind, making pretty good horses look as if they had just remembered a pressing engagement with the quarter pole.

He is not a great horse, in the sense that Man o' War and Equipoise were great. He isn't versatile. There are dozens of horses around that can beat him at a mile, and even at a mile and a quarter he would have trouble with Armed or Lucky Draw, just as he had trouble with Devil Diver. He can't make his own pace and he can't win slow races. He needs something up ahead to draw the speed from the field, to soften it up for his long, sweeping rush at the end.

But give him a field with speed in it, at a mile and a half or more, and horses had better get out of his way, even Whirlaway.

Anyway, another fine and ardent and satisfactory story of the turf was brought to a close at Jamaica. And it was happy to note that, for all the long campaign, it was not battered and limping warrior which left us. Stymie never looked better with his bronze coat in great bloom, and the high head carried as proudly as ever.

As he stood for the last time, before the stands, people around the winner's enclosure were shouting to his groom, "Bring him in here, for just one more time."

The groom didn't obey, and probably was right. Stymie never got in a winner's circle without working for it. It was no time to begin.

# The Greatest Tennis Player of All Time

## Allison Danzig

Back in the dark ages before television made tennis nationally
popular, the New York *Times* was the only American newspaper
giving the sport extensive and expert coverage. During the
forty-five years between 1923 and 1968 when Allison Danzig
served as the *Times* tennis reporter, he was often the only
American sportswriter on the scene when something big was
happening at Wimbledon or at the Roland Garros Stadium in
Paris, or on the courts at Sydney or Melbourne. Having seen all
the great ones, he is eminently qualified to select the greatest
tennis player of all time. Incidentally, this appraisal of Bill
Tilden was made in 1962, after Allison had watched a lot of
others come and go.

William Tatem Tilden II was his name. He was not only the
supreme, the most complete, tennis player of all time; he was also
one of the most colorful and controversial figures that the world of
sports has known.

His flair for the theatrical stemmed from a fascination with the
stage that had held him since boyhood. He would have given his
right arm, and his racket with it, to have been a successful,
idolized actor. Instead he was almost the worst who ever played on
Broadway, and he squandered the fortune he made from tennis
backing himself in stock companies and Broadway stage produc-
tions.

So to Tilden, a tall, gaunt figure with hulking shoulders and the
leanest of shanks, the tennis court became a stage. He was in love

with it and with the crowds before whom he performed. Most of the time the crowds were against him, or at least for his opponent, the underdog. To win them to his side, Tilden went to lengths that seemed to border on lunacy. He would allow his opponent to gain so big a lead as to make his own defeat appear inevitable. Then, from this precarious position, he would launch a spectacular comeback that had the crowd cheering him and that invariably ended with an ovation from the stands.

Only Tilden would have dared to set the stage as he did to make himself the hero instead of the villain. In 1925, he played Howard Kinsey for the Illinois State Championship at the Skokie Country Club in Glencoe. Kinsey was then the fourth ranking player in the country, and the national doubles champion with his brother Robert. After winning the first two sets, Tilden lost the next two. Leading 2–0 in the fifth set, he then lost the next five games. The crowd of 5,000 buzzed with excitement. Could it be that the great Tilden was going down in defeat?

The court was close to Lake Michigan and a cold wind was blowing. The crowd was bundled in coats and blankets. As the players changed sides, with Tilden trailing, 2–5, he took off his sweater for the first time in the match, picked up a pitcher of ice water at the umpire's chair and poured it over his head.

A shiver went through the crowd. Tilden carefully dried his head and hands. Finally, he walked to the base line and prepared to serve. Then, adding to the suspense, he beckoned to a ball boy to bring him a towel with the imperious gesture he used so often before his tennis audiences. Meticulously, he wiped a last bit of moisture from his hands. By now the gallery was limp from tension.

With the stage set, Tilden picked up his racket and the balls and cut loose. Kinsey could only win one more game. Final score: Tilden, 8–6. The cheers for Big Bill at the end were wild.

This ability of Tilden's to extricate himself from seemingly hopeless situations (deliberately arrived at), even against players far superior to Kinsey, was a manifestation of his unrivaled supremacy. To establish that he ranks above all other tennis players

of all time, it is necessary to examine his attributes—his physical
and mental capacities and stroke ability—and the abilities of his
contemporaries.

In such sports as track and swimming it is easy enough to
compare athletes of different generations by citing time records.
In tennis, as in prizefighting, there are no such yardsticks. The
only arguments are how much punch the athlete had with his right
or left fist, or with his forehand or backhand, and how good were
the men he beat.

Tilden held absolute sway in a period when there were probably
more first class tennis players than either before or since. In the
1920s, France, Spain and Japan produced their most renowned
players. The French had Henri Cochet, Rene Lacoste, and Jean
Borotra and Jacques Brugnon. Australia had Gerald Patterson,
with a devastating service and overhead smash, and Jim Anderson
with a rifle forehand. Here in our own country there were "Little
Bill" Johnston, who might have won the national championship
eight times instead of twice (1915 and 1919) if his career had not
coincided with Tilden's, and Vincent Richards, another player of
the first class. Johnston ranks among the half dozen top players of
all time. Richards had no superior as a volleyer. He had extraordi-
nary control of the ball, even in returning Tilden's cannonball
service.

These players were mastered by Tilden when he reigned as the
national champion from 1920 through 1925, won every one of his
twelve Davis Cup challenge-round matches in singles and carried
off the Wimbledon crown both times that he competed for it. He
was their master for the following reasons:

(1) He had the greatest combination forehand and backhand
drive the game has ever known. No other player could hit with
such pace and control from both sides. Donald Budge's backhand
is usually rated today ahead of all others, but not by those who saw
Tilden in his prime.

With his great strength in the fundamental strokes and his zest
for moving his opponent about, he preferred to stay in the back
court rather than rush to the net. There are those, therefore, who

mistakenly assert that he could not volley. Tilden was not the equal of Johnston or Richards at the net, nor was he as strong overhead as would have been expected of so tremendous a server, but when he chose to, or had to, go in, he was a master of the drop volley, as he was of the drop shot.

(2) His service ranks with the greatest. His first serve was as consistently fast as any with the possible exception of Ellsworth Vines's and the frequency with which he could make the chalk fly on the center line when he was behind was discouraging to his opponents. There have been few American twist services to compare in "kick" with his second ball.

(3) He was unrivalled as a student and master of spin. He could blow his opponent off the court with pace or he could break down the other player's control with a chop or a slice used alternately with a flat or top-spin drive.

(4) No player had a better physique for the game. Tilden stood 6 foot 1 and weighed 165 pounds; he had broad shoulders, a lean waistline and long, tapering legs that carried him swiftly with giant strides. Invariably he was in perfect condition and could battle interminably, despite the fact that he smoked incessantly off the court and ate prodigious amounts of food an hour or two before playing.

(5) No other player moved more gracefully or with footwork that was more secure. His speed has hardly been excelled except by Fred Perry's, and no matter how fast he ran, or how far he reached, he rarely made a shot off balance.

(6) There has never been a more thorough student of the game or a greater master of tactics. This is evidenced not only by his craft on the court but also in his writings, particularly in his classic work, *Match Play and Spin of the Ball*.

(7) No player ever loved the game more, got more pleasure from the play or gave his life to tennis more wholeheartedly than did Tilden, from the age of 7 until he died at 60 in 1953.

It is also true that there was never a more temperamental player than Tilden, nor one more opinionated. He was a supreme egoist, although off the court he could be gracious and charming. He had a deep love of music acquired from his mother. He had friends devoted to him—among them Mary Garden, the opera singer, and Mrs. Molla Bjurstedt Mallory, seven times the winner of the women's national singles tennis championship, and a woman of great courage and pride.

On the court, too, Tilden could be winning and generous. But he could also be carping, demanding and fault-finding to a point where the gallery turned against him. Linesmen and ball boys were often the objects of his ire. At the Orange Lawn Tennis Club in New Jersey, where the turf was as good as any in the country, he informed the chairman that he was not accustomed to playing in a cow pasture. At the Westchester Country Club in Rye, New York, he was losing badly to Clifford Sutter in a quarter-final match of the 1930 Eastern grass court championship tournament. The gallery was on him for his poor tennis and his temperamental displays. Finally a woman in the stands shouted at him, "Play tennis!" In a rage he walked off the court and defaulted.

Old-timers who saw Tilden at his peak still hold to the belief that he was the greatest player the world has ever seen. Those of the same generation who may give preference to Budge, Kramer, Vines, Gonzales or Perry or some other will respect the choice of Tilden while arguing rationally for their own man. Not so the younger generation who saw Tilden, if at all, in the late stages of his career.

To the young players currently active it is like waving a red flag before a bull to suggest that Tilden, or any other player of his time, would have a ghost of a chance against Gonzales, Kramer, Hoad or some of the other modern-day champions who play the Big Game. Nobody can convince them that Tilden would not now be hopelessly outdated and outclassed.

They maintain flatly that the game of the Big Serve and Volley came in with Kramer and Ted Schroeder and they point out that it was Australia's changing to this type of play after taking a series of bad lickings from the United States in the Davis Cup matches of the late 1940s that put the boys from Down Under up yonder.

The fact is that tennis was played identically in Tilden's time as it is today, except that there were not as many net rushers and the rallies were longer. There was never a more daring game than that played by Dick Williams, who went in on his big serve and made most of his subsequent shots on the half-volley or the full volley when he won the national championships in 1914 and 1916. Who ever rushed the net more often than Jean Borotra or Wilmer Allison?

Tilden was supreme over the great volleyers and servers until 1926, and at times defeated them years later, primarily because of the strength of his ground strokes. He could return the Big Serve wrathfully and he repulsed the volleyer with passing shots from either side. It would be the same for him today, if he was playing at his prime against Big Game players, as it was 40 years ago.

Ellsworth Vines said in 1958 that he always considered Tilden the greatest tennis player. In 1934, when Tilden was 41 years old and Vines was 22, they met in a professional match in Los Angeles. Vines finally won after a three hour battle, 6–0, 21–23, 7–5, 3–6, 6–2. Wilmer Allison has written:

"I have gotten tired of hearing people, who should know better, saying that Tilden wasn't the greatest that ever lived. I never played Tilden when he was at his best, but I did play against him five years later, in the finals at Wimbledon in 1930 and, in all of the time that I played, I never felt so helpless as I did that day. Of course I haven't played Hoad or Gonzales, but I did play Vines, Budge, Perry and Kramer. They were great players, but they certainly weren't the equal of Tilden."

Frank Hunter, who was Tilden's partner in the U.S. and Wimbledon doubles championships and on Davis Cup teams, and who was twice a runner-up for the national singles title, has summed it up this way:

"Tilden could have changed his game if necessary and could have played the Big Game. He could play any kind of game. He had a wonderfully analytical mind in sizing up the other fellow, his strengths and weaknesses, and deciding what methods and tactics to use. He had the equipment to beat them all—past and present. There's never been anyone like him."

# The Iceman Cometh

## Stan Fischler

Eddie Shore was the toughest, and probably the best, defenseman in the National Hockey League, and the most booed and
applauded player of his time. When he came from Edmonton to
join the Boston Bruins in 1929, Shore lifted the club from last
place to second place in the league's American Division and
filled every seat in the new Boston Garden. Hammy Moore, the
Bruins' trainer in the 1930s, once said, "Shore was the only
player I ever saw who would bring the whole crowd to its feet
every time he carried the puck down the ice. You could be sure
he would end up scoring a goal or getting into a fight." He ended
his career in 1940 with a total of 978 stitches in his body,
fourteen nose fractures, five jaw fractures, and four awards as
the league's most valuable player of the year. This remarkable
account of one of his memorable adventures shows you why so
many old-timers claim that there has never been another hockey
player like Eddie Shore.

On January 2, 1929, the Boston Bruins boarded a night train to
Montreal for a National Hockey League game there the following
evening against the Montreal Maroons. As the train was pulling
out of the North Station, Art Ross, the Bruins' manager, walked
through the Pullman sleeping car, counting the players. When
Ross reached the last berth, he realized that one of them, Eddie
Shore, was missing.

"Ross didn't know it," Shore said recently, "but I was then
running down the platform trying to jump on the last car of the
train. I didn't make it. I just missed the train because my taxi got
tied up in a traffic accident coming across town."

Shore was determined to get to Montreal in time for the game.

The Bruins were already shorthanded because of injuries, and Shore was well aware that Ross levied a $500 fine on any player who missed a road trip. Shore checked the train schedule and found that the next express to Montreal in the morning would not reach there until after the game had started. He learned that all of the airline planes were grounded because of stormy weather. He was about to rent an automobile when a wealthy Boston friend offered to lend him a limousine with a chauffeur. At 11:30 that night Shore and the chauffeur started the 350-mile drive north over iced and snow-blocked New England mountain roads. It was sleeting, and in those days there were no paved express highways, no sanding trucks and no road patrols. The chauffeur drove very slowly through the storm. "I was not happy about the way he was driving," Shore said, "and I told him so. He apologized and said he didn't have chains and didn't like driving in the winter. The poor fellow urged me to turn back to Boston."

At that point the car skidded to the lip of a ditch. Shore took over at the wheel and drove to an all-night service station where he had tire chains put on. By then the sleet storm had thickened into a blizzard. Snow caked either side of the lone windshield wiper, and within minutes the wiper blade froze solid to the glass. "I couldn't see out the window," says Shore, "so I removed the top half of the windshield."

His face was exposed to the blasts of the icy wind and snow but he managed to see the road. At about 5 A.M., in the mountains of New Hampshire, "we began losing traction. The tire chains had worn out."

Slowly, Shore eased the car around a bend in the road where he could see the lights of a construction camp flickering. He awakened a gas station attendant there, installed a new set of chains and weaved on. "We skidded off the road four times," he says, "but each time we managed to get the car back on the highway again."

The second pair of chains fell off at three the next afternoon. This time Shore stopped the car and ordered the chauffeur to take over the wheel. "I felt that a short nap would put me in good shape," he says. "All I asked of the driver was that he go at least twelve miles an hour and stay in the middle of the road."

But the moment Shore dozed off, the chauffeur lost control of the big car and it crashed into a deep ditch. Neither Shore nor the chauffeur nor the car suffered any damage so Shore hiked a mile to a farmhouse for help. "I paid $8 for a team of horses," says Shore, "harnessed the horses and pulled the car out of the ditch. We weren't too far from Montreal and I thought we'd make it in time if I could keep the car on the road."

He did and at 5:30 P.M. Shore drove up to the Windsor Hotel, the Bruins' headquarters. He staggered into the lobby and nearly collapsed. "He was in no condition for hockey," says Ross. "His eyes were bloodshot, his face frostbitten and windburned, his fingers bent and set like claws after gripping the steering wheel so long. And he couldn't walk straight. I figured his legs were almost paralyzed from hitting the brake and clutch."

Nevertheless Shore ate a steak dinner, his first real meal in twenty-four hours, and refused the coach's orders to go to sleep. "I was tired all right," Shore says, "but I thought a twenty- or thirty-minute nap would be enough, then I'd be set to play."

An hour later Dit Clapper and Cooney Weiland of the Bruins entered Shore's room and shook him gently. Nothing happened. They rolled him over the bed and onto the floor. Still nothing happened. Weiland filled several glasses with water and poured them over Shore's face. This time he woke up and immediately insisted on playing.

Ross didn't want him to play. "I knew how durable he was," the coach says, "but there's a limit to human endurance. I finally decided to let him get on the ice, but at the first sign of weakness or sleepwalking I'd send him to the dressing room. I had to worry about him being groggy. What if he got hit hard and wound up badly hurt?"

The game was rough and fast. The powerful Maroons penetrated Boston's defense often, but Shore always helped repulse them. He smashed Hooley Smith to the ice with a vicious body check and drew the game's first penalty. Ross considered benching him at this point, but changed his mind. When the penalty had elapsed, Shore jumped on the ice and appeared stronger than ever. Shortly before the halfway point in the second period he skated behind his net to retrieve the puck. He faked one Montreal player, picked up speed at center ice and swerved to the left when he reached the Maroons' blue line. He sped around the last defenseman and shot. "I would say I was fifteen feet out to the left," he says. "I can remember exactly how my shot went. It was low, about six inches off the ice, and went hard into the right corner of the net." The time of the goal was 8:20 of the second period. The Bruins led 1–0.

Shore still showed no signs of his ordeal during the third period (he had another two-minute penalty), and almost twenty-four hours after he had chased the train down the North Station platform in Boston the final buzzer sounded. Apart from the two penalties, Shore had played the entire game without relief and, what's more, had scored the only goal of the game. Coach Ross never fined him for missing the train.

# Antonino the Great

## Robert O'Brien

Wrestling, when it is conducted honestly by school and college
teams, must be the dullest sport for a spectator to watch. Modern professional wrestling, of course, isn't a sport at all—it may
be described as a melodramatic freak show with a cast of gri-
macing musclemen, bleached-blond monsters, and blubbery
buffoons acting as outraged heroes and dastardly villains. But
putting aside the ethical questions, here is an engrossing close-
up study of an athlete who has attracted wildly applauding sell-
out crowds in such places as Madison Square Garden, the Olympic Auditorium in Los Angeles, the American Legion Arena
in Teaneck, New Jersey, and the Knights of Columbus Hall in
Bridgeport, Connecticut, not to mention Luna Park in Buenos
Aires and Ridgewood Grove in Brooklyn.

Sometimes on Monday nights in the winter Madison Square Garden sold out very fast and early, and thousands of Puerto Ricans
were left out in Eighth Avenue, shivering in the icy wind and filled
with misery because they could not see their idol, Antonino
Rocca, wrestle.

One Monday in 1959, it was different. Many Manhattan wrestling fans seemed to have other things to do that evening, so the
Puerto Ricans swarmed into the arena and took nearly all of the
18,000 seats, from ringside all the way back into the reaches of the
upper galleries.

When two peroxide blonds in spangled blue capes entered the
ring for the main match, a storm of boos and catcalls filled the
Garden's vastness. The wrestlers wore their hair bobbed. Their
skin was milk-white. They looked out of condition. They ankled
around the ring, swaying their hips and making the crowd howl.

Rocca and his tag-team partner, Miguel Perez, moved swiftly down the aisle. They bounded into the ring. The crowd greeted them with an exultant shout. Rocca wore dark trunks and a red cardigan sweater. He was barefoot. Perez wore white trunks, white shoes and a white sweater. Rocca is a man in his thirties. His head is too large and his legs too short for his body. He carries his head lowered and thrust forward. His hair is dark and cropped short. He has a mashed right ear and a large curving nose and a big chin. Perez is younger. He is tall and rangy, built like an oarsman.

Antonino and Miguel watched quietly while the two blond heavyweights strutted about preposterously like ham actors playing Nero. The announcer, first in English, then in Spanish, awarded Rocca and Perez two glittering gold-plated trophies—*Ring* magazine's award to the tag team which did the most for wrestling in 1958. In a tag-team match, there are two wrestlers to a side. They take turns performing in the ring.

Rocca and Perez handed the trophies over the ropes to their manager and peeled off their sweaters. Rocca danced lightly up and down. The announcer began the introductions. One of the blonds leaned out over the ropes, jeering at somebody in the crowd. Rocca lunged at him and smashed him in the face three times with the heel of his right hand.

The crowd screamed. Rocca's head, arms, legs and torso, seeming so mismated in repose, suddenly blended into fluid, beautifully balanced components, moving in smooth, controlled, animal grace. He leaped high in the air, crossed the ring in a series of bouncing handsprings, waving his arms, bellowing, and whipping the crowd into a frenzy of excitement.

The bell clanged. The match began, with Perez, Rocca's partner, taking the ring for his team. He absorbed a punishing series of monkey flips, sling shots, body slams, arm locks, flying·mares, forearm chops and eye gouges. He reeled groggily around the ring. The crowd roared. Then, amazingly, Perez recovered. He hit his blond opponent in the face with one forearm smash after another. The blond fell to his knees and begged for mercy.

The match was for two out of three falls, and Rocca and Perez won the first fall after nine minutes. Perez was pinned to the mat and lost the second fall after twelve minutes. The end came fourteen minutes later in a wild melee that began when one of the blonds connected with a forearm chop to Rocca's head. Rocca staggered to a corner and reached for the ropes. Again the blond's elbow smashed to his skull. Rocca slipped down helplessly to the middle rope. His head wobbled. The crowd was frantic. Suddenly Rocca came back to life. He vaulted to the blond's shoulders and perched there like a giant gargoyle. He anchored himself, with his heels under the blond's arms, and brought his fist down on top of the blond's head. "Kill him, Rocca!" the crowd yelled. "Kill him, Antonino!"

Rocca sprang off the blond's shoulders to the canvas. Leaping up, he shot his bare feet against his opponent's chest. The blond sprawled to the mat. Both men got back on their feet and circled each other. Rocca kicked out again with his feet, and again and again. With each kick, the crowd roared. At the last kick, his opponent fell backward. Rocca pounced on him and pinned his back to the canvas. The referee slapped the mat three times, signifying that the match was over. Rocca and Perez had won again.

A fight started in the crowd near the ringside. A dozen policemen converged on it. Rocca, wearing his red sweater, stepped to the microphone and appealed for order, shouting, "Hey! Amigos—aqui!—momento! Show the people that you are gentlemen!" The Garden's organist began to play "The Star-Spangled Banner." The blond wrestlers disappeared. Rocca and Perez stood in the ring with the announcer, singing the national anthem. The shouting died down. The crowd stood at attention. When the music stopped, the people streamed to the exits and out into the soft night air. Their eyes were shining. Their faces were happy. Whether it had been real, or not, didn't matter to them. It had been a wonderful show and a wonderful evening.

Antonino Rocca is one of the greatest single attractions in the sports world. He has broken attendance records in almost every sports arena from Buenos Aires to Montreal, from Boston to Lima, Peru. In 1958, when he wrestled eleven times in Madison Square Garden, seven of his appearances were sell-outs. Attendance at his matches that year totalled more than 200,000 and gate receipts were over $500,000. Run-of-the-mill wrestlers in the New York area may earn between $10,000 and $25,000 a year. Ten or twelve others—including a half dozen peroxided "queens of the mat"—may earn as much as $75,000 a year. Rocca pulls in around $180,000 to $200,000 a year, and has averaged more than $150,000 annually ever since he arrived in this country from Argentina ten years ago.

Rocca's working schedule would tax the stamina of an astronaut. He wrestles on the average of three nights a week, month in and month out. To meet these engagements, he travels 100,000 miles a year by air, and thousands of miles more by car. During a spell close to home, he may appear one night at the Garden, the next night in a theater in Harlem and the night after that at the American Legion Arena in Teaneck, New Jersey. More often he is hopping from one end of the country to the other. He has wrestled on a Saturday night in Burbank, California, on Monday in Madison Square Garden, on Tuesday in the Olympic Auditorium in Los Angeles, and, two nights later, at the Knights of Columbus Hall, Bridgeport, Connecticut.

Professional wrestling today is a combination of a grappling match, side show, tumbling exhibition, Pier Nine brawl and medieval morality play. The most popular matches are presented as conflicts between hero and villain, good and evil. In the interest of "showmanship," a galaxy of freaks has gathered on the wrestling scene: midgets, professional fat men, marcelled males whose minions spray the ring with cologne before a match, bearded Turks, mat-chested Tarzans from the jungles of Hoboken, narcissistic weight-lifters who strike poses and ripple their muscles at housewives who sit, hair in pin-curls, quivering in the ringside seats.

King of this carnival crew is Rocca. As the recognized champion of the downtrodden, the oppressed and the kicked-around minorities, Rocca, to millions of Americans, is a shining-hero image. He is the Siegfried of the slums, the hope of the hopeless, the Beowulf of the misbegotten. To the New York Puerto Ricans, his most fanatic admirers, he is even more—a big brother who has made good. Although he is not a Latin American by birth, he came to New York from South America, speaks Spanish, eats *arroz con pollo, paella,* and *asopato,* dances the Puerto Rican dances and sings sad Puerto Rican songs. He has done what the New York Puerto Rican dreams of doing—he has pitted himself against New York and has gotten money, cars, women, clothes, luxuries and prestige. And with all that he has won, he remains a simple hero with a simple heart.

So the Puerto Ricans stream from their tenements on San Juan Hill and East Harlem when he wrestles at the Garden. "Rocca makes us forget our troubles," one of them says. "He makes us laugh. He gives us hope. He is one of us. And he never loses."

Rocca, from infancy, has been something of a prodigy. He was born in Treviso, Italy, on April 13, 1926. The hospital staff could hardly believe its scales; he weighed one ounce over eighteen pounds. And he was followed into the world a few moments later by a twin sister who weighed nine pounds.

Antonino was the sixth child. His twin sister died of pneumonia when she was three months old and then his mother gave birth later to another baby. Antonino's growth became the talk of Treviso. At the age of six months, he weighed twenty-eight pounds, and when he was eight years old, he weighed 140 pounds. Even so, he recalled recently, on nights when he refused to go to bed, his mother would "grab me, pick me up and stick me under her arm, and carry me upstairs."

His mother, I remarked to him, must have been an Amazon.

"No," he said. "She was not large. But she had a very beautiful, well-balanced body."

Balance is the key to winning wrestling, Rocca contends. You must keep your balance, he says, and you must deprive your opponent of his balance. In fact, balance to him is everything. "You can do anything in this life if you have balance," he says. The other big element, he says, is quality, meaning "class," style, or heart. If a person has "quality," Rocca accepts him, but if somebody lacks quality, he does not interest Rocca. He will say of a wrestler who has fallen out of condition, "That fellow now is no good. He has let himself go. He no longer has quality."

Describing his childhood, Rocca sketched for me a picture of a poor but proud and closely-knit family living on a farm in the fertile flat country north of Venice. In the early 1930s, Antonino's two older brothers emigrated to Argentina and found work with a construction company in Rosario. A few years later Antonino joined them. He went to high school and to the university in Rosario, planning to become an electrical engineer. He was a natural athlete, an excellent high jumper and shot-putter and captain of his school's rugby team, tough, limber and fast on his feet. An international professional wrestling competition was staged in Buenos Aires. Although he had never seen professional wrestling, he was invited to join the tournament. "I was happy playing rugby and working for my engineering degree," he says, "but when I saw those wrestlers, crashing to the mat with everybody yelling and screaming, I wanted to jump into the ring with them."

Rocca's first opponent in the competition was Kola Kwariani, a 218-pound Georgian from Tbilisi, who represented the United States. A ponderous bear of a man, Kwariani had lost only four matches in twenty-one years of professional wrestling. "He threw me all over the ring for the first three or four minutes," Rocca recalls. "Then all at once I knew what to do. I gave him my knees in his face, elbows in his eyes and put him down and made him quit." Rocca won his next match, against Count Karol Nowina, a Polish star, in two minutes and then went on to win the championship. Kwariani invited him to become a professional, and, acting as his manager, booked him into Luna Park in Buenos Aires for twenty-six weeks before taking him on a tour of South America.

Even in the sometimes zombie world of wrestling, Kwariani was a picturesque figure. He spoke twelve languages fluently, had once operated a Left Bank restaurant in Paris, was an authority on Sudanese cooking and had won an international rating as a chess player. His voice was as thick as long-brewed borscht and full of guttural power and original phrases. Between Kwariani and Rocca there developed the relationship that flourishes between the wise old pro, full of lore and craft, and the raw but gifted protégé whom he is grooming for the big money. Rocca spent several years barnstorming in South America, growing tougher and more skillful. Then Joe ("Toots") Mondt, the American wrestling promoter, came to South America on a tour with Primo Carnera and watched Rocca perform in Rio de Janiero. Mondt and Kwariani worked out a co-managership deal. Two months later Rocca and Kwariani came to New York and Antonino made his North American debut at Ridgewood Grove in Brooklyn.

Kwariani observed recently that, in his judgment, Rocca is a universal man. "Rocca could be a great engineer, a great composer, a great poet," he said. "The only thing he could not be is a great boxer. He is too strong for that. He would punch so hard that he would break his hands, like Carpentier."

We were sitting in Kwariani's small bedroom in his apartment in a West Forties hotel. There were three telephones on the coffee table; he had been talking on them for hours. In addition to being the co-manager of Rocca, Kwariani is a matchmaker of wrestling bouts. It was three in the afternoon and he had not yet had time to get dressed. He sat on the edge of his unmade bed in his underwear, wearing gold-rimmed spectacles and looking like a Slavic Buddha. The apartment was being redecorated. Books were piled everywhere. An unframed oil portrait of Kwariani's lovely, dark wife, Sidonia, perched on the air conditioner, and there were dozens of other unframed oil paintings on the floor, facing the walls.

Kwariani told me about his first match with Rocca in Buenos Aires. "I wanted to show this young man something," he said. "I wanted him to respect me. For three or four minutes, I was beating him, tying him in knots. Then he started to move. He was suddenly like a reptile in my arms. He was suddenly made of elastic steel, all arms, all legs. All I had learned in twenty-one years of wrestling, he had learned in three minutes. I gave up. I was red from exertion. Rocca was not even pink. He was breathing easily, like a colt after a frolic in a meadow, and his face was aglow. He was a man who had found himself."

Kwariani said that Rocca has an ideal structure for a wrestler. He is not overdeveloped in the chest; most of his weight is from his waist down, in his legs. "He is built like a monkey," Kwariani said. "A monkey moves with the same dynamics as Rocca. He never wastes energy. He saves it for when it is needed. He can relax anytime. If I tell him to sleep for two hours, he sleeps for two hours. He designs his own holds, his own wrestling style. Every hold I tried to show when he was younger, he had no heart for. Once he said to me, 'Kola, allow me to demonstrate my own technique.' He gave me a kick in the chest and fractured my sternum. He was wearing shoes then. That is why he never wears them in the ring today, because he does not like to break anybody's bones."

It was necessary to teach Rocca to hold back and to restrain himself in the early stages of a match because, as Kwariani pointed out to him, if he defeated all of his opponents in less than seven minutes, no crowds would pay to watch him perform.

"One day I watched my wife's cat, Pushkin, playing with a mouse," Kwariani said. "That gave me an idea. I told Rocca not to use the body scissors and other big and winning holds unless the other man is his equal. At all other times, he must be Pushkin playing with the mouse. When the mouse ceased to be dynamic, stopped putting up a fight, Pushkin picked him up and brought him to me, a trophy. That is what I told Rocca to do. Be the cat, and when the other man ceases to be dynamic, beat him up quickly and give him to the crowd. I teach him to encourage his opponent to overconfidence. Then, when he senses that the crowd wants him to win, he wins."

Fifteen blocks from Kwariani's hotel, close to the tenement

district known as Hell's Kitchen, Rocca lives in a top floor apartment in a new and modern building with a sidewalk marquee and a
doorman on duty at all times. He has three rooms, a tiny kitchenette, a small bedroom with a large double bed and a closet
crammed with shoes, topcoats, odd jackets, slacks and suits almost
Ivy League enough in style to have come from Brooks Brothers,
and a long narrow living room with windows overlooking West
Fifty-seventh Street. It is furnished in new French Provincial.
Here there are touches of pure Rocca: the small Puerto Rican flag
sticking out of an alabaster vase on the French Provincial coffee
table; the humidor filled with Garcia y Vega cigars in glass tubes;
the sideboard that opens up to become a hi-fi radio and phono-
graph; the 400-day gilt clock on the sideboard beside a silk-shaded
lamp with crystal pendants and a gray and yellow stuffed rabbit;
wrestling trophies, gold-plated, with fluted columns and tiny
laurel-crowned figures of Greek athletes; an oil painting of Lake
Como, ornately framed; glassware, an automatic coffee maker and
three books, the Bible, *The Complete Works of Oscar Wilde* in
Spanish, and *The Kefauver Story.*

I visited Rocca's apartment several times, and accompanied him
from there to some of his matches and from there to the small Latin
American restaurant off Broadway where he goes after the wrestling. It was always a trip to another region, a region of incongru-
ities, and of people who, for all I knew, made their livings from
being shot from cannons. I could never quite believe that it was
real.

One evening I walked in to find Rocca in gray track pants, red
shirt and Japanese sandals, talking loudly with a small, worried-
looking man in a dark suit with a pencil-thin mustache. Rocca
introduced him as his friend, George Unger. On the floor, spilling
out of their packages and excelsior, were three automatic coffee
makers, a singing teakettle, a picnic jug, a bottle of Scotch and an
electric sander.

Rocca slapped me on the back. "My friend George has a store on
Forty-seventh Street," he said. "He has more bigness than anybody. He gave me these things to give to poor Puerto Ricans,

which I will do tomorrow. He has given me three thousand dollars worth of toys for the kids of Argentina, and twenty watches, in Braille, for blind people in Argentina who otherwise could not tell what time it is. George Unger, boy—a real American."

The night before a big match, Rocca deadens the bell on his telephone and sleeps until noon. He makes his own breakfast, fruit, cereal, toast and coffee. Once, when I arrived in time for breakfast coffee, I watched him eat seven slices of white toast lavishly spread with a fine, bitter English marmalade. After dressing, he descends to the lobby, gives the doorman a dollar bill and goes for a stroll. He is well known in the neighborhood and talks with everyone. He is always giving things away—cigars to old men, dimes and quarters to street urchins, postcard pictures of himself to teen-agers. "When I give things to people," he says, "I give away my tensions."

Rocca never observes a strict schedule. This comes from Kwariani, whom he calls "The Philosopher." The concept is that no man, even an athlete in training, should be rigid, or fanatic, about anything; it is important to remain relaxed, fluid. "No man," Rocca says, "should be a dictator. Most of all, he should not be a dictator over himself."

So anywhere between 2:30 and 4 o'clock in the afternoon, Rocca has his big meal of the day—meat, vegetables, fresh fruit—which he usually eats in a Greek restaurant down the street from his apartment house. Kwariani believes that sugar puts a wrestler in an aggressive mood: about 6 o'clock Rocca swallows several blockbuster vitamin pills made according to his own formula, and tops them off with a tall glass of concentrated grape juice or orange juice mixed with honey. Then he relaxes in a sweat suit, listening to music, until it is time to leave for the match. He sits forward alertly on the edge of his chair, smokes a cigar and looks around happily.

A flag waves from a housetop pole across the street. "Goddam, boy—look at that beautiful flag," Rocca says. "It gives me an injection of happiness. Everything is beautiful. Even that chimney, blowing smoke into the sky, has poetry." He puffs his cigar. "Goddam, boy—what a country this is. She has got everything.

People go to Switzerland to see the Alps; Rocky Mountains is better. People go to South America for vacation; Key Largo is better. Why don't they stay home? I will tell you." He taps his forehead. "No brains."

Rocca likes people. He takes a lively interest in them and their troubles. He is always ready with an observation, a bit of philosophy, to weave a friend's anecdote into the larger fabric of life.

One evening, before a tag-team match against the Graham Brothers at the Garden, a friend named Alejandro was at the apartment with a crippled youth of eighteen or nineteen, named Carlos. Alejandro was a slender man in his late thirties, a Spanish film producer whose movies had won several prizes. Carlos, a blue-eyed Argentinean in a cardigan sweater, sat in a French Provincial chair with his left leg in a steel brace. Both of his arms and hands were withered. He had been a cripple since birth and had come to the United States for corrective surgery. He had already undergone seven operations. He spoke English hesitantly but clearly, and he was smoking one of Rocca's Garcia y Vega cigars. You could see that he was happy with the cigar, but it kept going out and he kept relighting it, with difficulty, with a cigarette lighter in his twisted hands.

Rocca sat listening to Alejandro, who was recounting the marital troubles of a friend.

"It is the end," Alejandro said. "He cannot stand her any longer. Before they were married, she was telling him all the time how handsome he was and what brilliance he had, what intelligence. Then they are married. Overnight he becomes a stupid pig. Now he is afraid of her. He takes her her meals to eat in the bed. She speaks, and he trembles. He is miserable. It cannot go on."

Rocca leans forward, elbows on knees. His estranged wife and their six-year-old daughter live in South America.

"Very sad," he said. "But"—he sighed in resignation—"is typical. A woman can destroy you. Is worse than guns. Gun is clean. One shot—boom!—that is all, that's the end, let's go. But a woman hounds you twenty-four hours a day. She drags out the death of the heart. She keeps tearing at it."

Alejandro looked unhappy. Carlos' young face lost its smile.

Rocca suddenly slapped his thighs and jumped up. "Let me make some coffee. I am a great technician at coffee." He went to the kitchenette. We heard running water and Rocca singing, "Amapola."

"All fighters," Alejandro said to me, "are a little of brutes." He stood up, hunched his shoulders and swung his arms like an ape. "All fighters but Antonino. He is the only delicate fighter. I cannot tell you how much he is this way." He held out his open hand, to signify giving. "Antonino is like a priest. He goes in the middle of the night to help people in trouble. If someone needs him, he is there. Yet he is like a child. Everybody likes Antonino—"

Carlos nodded eagerly. "He is strong for me—you understand? When I see him in the ring, I become Rocca. He gives me the feeling that I am living in the ring with him. I am big and strong. I am a conqueror. My legs are jumping with him."

Rocca came in with the strong, aromatic Colombian coffee, and while he was pouring it, he said, "My friends, what is the secret of happiness? It is to get up in the morning with a smile. To get up with responsibility, with the desire to do something worthwhile."

One evening, Rocca said, he came home from a bout in Denver. It was late, after midnight. He was tired from the flight and he was booked for the next night at St. Nick's. Before he could switch off the telephone bell, it rang. Kola. An old man, an Italian in The Bronx, wanted to see Rocca. "I am tired," Rocca said. "I must sleep."

"You must go," Kola said.

The old man's son came and picked Rocca up in a car. Rocca slept all the way to The Bronx. The old man was in bed. His wife had died of cancer two weeks earlier and now he did not want to live. He was refusing to eat. Two of the old man's sons took Rocca to the bedroom. "Father," one of them said, "we have brought Rocca, as we promised."

The old man could not believe that it was Rocca. Rocca stood there dazed. What could he do? Without any plan in mind, he said to the sons, "Leave us alone." When the sons had gone, he went to the old man's bedside. "Old man, life is beautiful," he said. "You are going to live."

"I am going to die," the old man said. "My strength is gone."

Rocca pulled off his coat, then his shirt, then his undershirt, and sat on a chair next to the bed, stripped to the waist.

"Put your hand on my chest," Rocca said. "Feel the heart of Rocca beating." The old man did so. "Can you hear what it says, old man? It says, 'Live! Live! Be a man!' "

The old man started to weep. "I want to, but I am too weak," he said. Rocca took the old man's hands between his own two big hands. He tried to will his vitality and strength to flow into the old man. Tears streamed down the old man's cheeks. Rocca himself began to weep.

The old man fell forward into Rocca's arms. "I will live!" he sobbed. "If you want me to, I will live!"

An hour later, when Rocca left the house, the old man was sitting up in bed, laughing and crying with his sons. He is alive to this day.

"We live in the big hand of God," Rocca said. "When he drops us, we must go. But until then, we must have joy of living."

One Friday evening there were matches in Paterson, New Jersey. Rocca and I went to the garage in the basement of his apartment building. Rocca carried his Abercrombie & Fitch kit bag, containing his red sweater, his dark wrestling trunks and his towels. We got into his black Chrysler Imperial, and Rocca headed up the West Side Highway to the George Washington Bridge. He drove fast and handled the powerful car tenderly. He managed to find a *malagueña* on the car's radio. The toll collector at the New Jersey end of the bridge grinned at him and said, "Hi, Rocca." Rocca headed off the bridge to Highway 4 and I talked with him about what he tried to do when he was in the wrestling ring. He switched off the radio.

"You put a guy in a position to smile," he said, "and that is greatness. In the ring, I try to transmit the desire to smile. My friend, some people find happiness in church, some in horses, some in rum or tequila, some with their wives and kids, and some in wrestling matches where they can yell and shout and call the referee a bum, and forget their troubles. I try to give them the dream that they are living with me in the ring and winning at all times. I want everybody to have a young face with a big smile."

The fans, after a match, are always waiting for him. I remember one night at a theater far uptown in Spanish Harlem. It seemed like a long time after the last match before Rocca appeared from backstage. Three people met him almost halfway up the aisle of the almost deserted theater; a woman in her thirties with a little girl of four or five, and a plain girl in her twenties in a threadbare coat and no hat.

The woman pushed the little girl forward. "This is my daughter, Mr. Rocca," she said. "She is little, but she is your good friend." Rocca squatted, and talked to the child. She stuck her finger in her mouth and rolled her eyes bashfully at her mother. Rocca chucked her under the chin. "What a little princess," he said.

As he stood up, the girl in the coat clutched his wrist. Her eyes were shining, and as she looked up at him something, some swift flame of hope and pride and fervor, came alight and alive in the drab aisle of the theater. "*Gana,* Rocca!" she said in a choked voice. "*Gana!*" She turned and hastened up the aisle after the departing mother and child.

"What did she say?" I asked him. "What does *gana* mean?"

"It means, 'Win, Rocca! Win! Conquer!' "

At St. Nick's, I had seen young Puerto Rican brides thrust at Rocca pictures of themselves in bridal gowns and ask him to autograph the picture in ink across its front, "To Lupe, from Antonino Rocca," "To Eva, from Antonino Rocca." Groups of teen-aged boys, most of them neat, clean and well-behaved, crowded around with glossy prints of Rocca in wrestling poses that they had bought in Harlem cigar stores or stationery shops.

While driving downtown, I asked him how long he was going to keep on wrestling.

"My friend," he said, "I am a great improvisor. I follow the curve of the situation. If your blood circulation is good and your reflexes are good, you can win matches. Perhaps I will wrestle for five, ten more years. Who knows? We live in the big hand of God."

We left the West Side Highway and drifted off south into the West Forties and pulled up in front of the Rancho Grande. It is a small Latin American bar and restaurant with photographs of Cuban and Puerto Rican baseball players and boxers on the walls. A dozen customers sat at the bar and in the booths, and all heads turned toward Rocca. There was good-natured banter in Spanish. Patsy, the manager, led us to a booth near the tiny orchestra platform.

"People know me here," Rocca said. "It is like home."

He ordered Champion Steak à la Rocca and a big salad and a bottle of a dry Cuban beer called Cristal.

Rocca smiled. "This is the life, no, my friend?" he said, and lighted a cigar. He waved to the musicians. They flashed their teeth and played more loudly. Rocca laughed.

"Music elevates me," he said. "Arturo Toscanini was my friend. He said, 'When you wrestle, you give me something like a symphony.' Wrestling is to me like a symphony. I feel music inside me when I wrestle."

The musicians began to play a quick, lively, rippling tune. Rocca rose smiling, chest out, and put down his cigar. "This is gaucho music," he said. "I play the maracas, and I forget everything."

He went to the bandstand, picked up the drummer's maracas and shook them expertly, adding their dry, shifting rhythm to the music. A young Puerto Rican and his girl friend joined Rocca at the bandstand, tapping out the beat with spoons against the sides of empty Coke bottles. The people at the bar looked on, smiling. They were getting into Rocca's mood. Some of them began to sing the Spanish words of the song.

Rocca threw his big head back and laughed. "Play!" he shouted to the musicians. "Play, *amigos!*"

# Bradley's Last
# Game for Princeton
## *John McPhee*

Basketball is often exciting to watch but, like hockey, its fast
action is not easy to describe on a typewriter. A rare accom-
plishment in sportswriting is this shot-by-shot description of Bill
Bradley's all-out scoring spree during his last game for Princeton
against Wichita in the final of the National Collegiate championship tournament in 1965. It is an excerpt from a *New Yorker*
profile of Bradley, written by one of his close friends at Princeton, John McPhee, and later expanded into a fascinating book, *A
Sense of Where You Are*, which was published by Farrar, Straus
& Giroux.

The Princeton-Wichita game ended, as a contest, when it had only
been underway for about five minutes and the score was Princeton
16, Wichita 4. The score at half time was Princeton 53, Wichita 39,
and later, with nine minutes and some seconds to go, it was 84 to
58.

Princeton's Coach van Breda Kolff began to take out his first
team players, leaving Bradley in the game. Bradley hit a short one
after taking the tap from a jump ball. He made two foul shots and a
jumper from the top of the key. He put in two more foul shots,
committed his own fourth personal foul, and looked toward van
Breda Kolff in expectation of leaving the game; but van Breda Kolff
ignored him. Getting the ball moments later, Bradley passed off to
Don Roth. Smiling and shaking his head slightly, Roth returned
the ball to Bradley.

There was a time-out and Bradley could hear people in the grandstands shouting at him that he ought to shoot when he got the ball. All of his teammates crowded around him and urged him to let it fly and not worry about anyone else on the floor. Van Breda Kolff, calmly enough, pointed out to him that his college career was going to end in less than five minutes and this was his last chance just to have a gunner's go at the basket for the sheer fun of it. "So," remembers Bradley, "I figured I might as well shoot."

In the next four minutes and forty-six seconds, Bradley changed almost all of the important records of national championship basketball. The most intense concentration of basketball people to collect anywhere at any given year is of course at the national championships, and as a group they stood, not quite believing, and smiling with pleasure at what they were seeing. Bradley, having decided to do as everyone was urging him to do, went into the left-hand corner and set up a long, high hook shot. "I'm out of my mind," he said to himself, but the shot dropped through the net. "O.K.," he thought, moving back up the court, "I'm going to shoot until I miss."

A moment later, sprinting up the floor through the Wichita defense, he took a perfect pass, turned slightly in the air, and tossed the ball over his shoulder and into the basket, with his left hand. The thirteen thousand people in the crowd, Wichita's huge mission of fans included, reacted with an almost unbelievable roar to each shot as it went into the basket. It was an individual performer's last and in some ways greatest moment. Everyone in the coliseum knew it, and, to Bradley, the atmosphere was tangible. "There would be a loud roar," he remembered, "then it was as if everyone were gathering their breath." Taking a pass at the base line, he jumped above a defender, extended his arm so that the shot would clear the backboard, and sent a sixteen-foot jumper into the basket. Someone in the crowd started to chant, "I believe! I believe!" and others took it up, until, after each shot, within the overall clamor, the amusing chant could be heard.

From the left side, Bradley went up for a jump shot. A Wichita player was directly in front of him, in the air, too, ready to block it. Bradley had to change the position of the ball, and, all in a second, let it go. He was sure that it was not going to go in, but it did. Coming up the floor again, he stopped behind the key and hit another long jumper from there. Within the minute, he had the ball again and was driving upcourt with it, but a Wichita player stayed with him, and forced him into the deep right-hand corner. Suddenly he saw that he was about to go out of bounds, so he jumped in the air and—now really convinced that he was out of his mind—released a twenty-two-foot hook shot, which seemed to him to be longer and more haphazard than any hook shot he had ever taken and certain to miss. It dropped through the net. Thirty seconds later he drove into the middle, stopped, faked, and hit a short, clean jumper. Twenty seconds after that he had the ball again and went high into the air on the right side of the court to execute, perfectly, the last shot of his college career. With thirty-three seconds left in the game, van Breda Kolff took him out.

Princeton had beaten Wichita 118 to 82 and had scored more points than any other team in any other game in the history of the national championships, a record which had previously been set and reset in opening rounds of play. Bradley had scored fifty-eight points, breaking Oscar Robertson's individual scoring record, which had been set in a regional consolation game. Hitting twenty-two shots from the floor, he had also broken Robertson's field goal record. His one hundred and seventy-seven points made in the tournament against Penn State, North Carolina State, Providence, Michigan, and Wichita were the most ever made by any player in the course of the national championships, breaking by seventeen points the record held by Jerry West of West Virginia and Hal Lear of Temple. His sixty-five field goals in five games set a record, too. His team had also scored more points across the tournament than any other team ever had, breaking a record set six years earlier by West Virginia. It had made forty-eight field goals against Wichita, breaking a record set by U.C.L.A.; and it made one hundred and seventy-three field goals in the tournament, twenty-one more than Loyola of Illinois made in 1963 while setting the previous-record and winning the national championship.

In his final nine minutes of play in the Wichita game, Bradley had scored twenty-six points, missing once, and had set seven records. After van Breda Kolff and the others had persuaded him to forget his usual standards and to shoot every time he got the ball, he had scored—in less than five minutes—sixteen points without missing a shot.

Conquerors of this sort usually follow up their homecoming with a lingering parade through the streets of Rome, but Bradley disappeared less than twenty-four hours after his return to Princeton, having arranged to live alone in a house whose owners were away. Far enough away from the campus to be cut off from it almost completely, he stayed there for a month—while a couple of hundred reporters, photographers, ministers, missionaries, Elks, Rotarians, Lions, TV producers, mayors, ad men, and fashion editors tried unsuccessfully to find him. Bradley went into seclusion in order to write his senior thesis, and, working about fifteen hours a day for thirty days, he completed it. The thesis was thirty-three thousand words long, and he finished it one month to the day after the game with Wichita. It received a straight 1—grades at Princeton begin with 1 and end with 7—and Bradley was graduated with honors.